Eyes Open on a World

Eyes Open on a World

The Challenges of Change

A Collaboration by the
Sisters of St. Joseph of Carondelet
St. Paul Province

NORTH STAR PRESS OF ST. CLOUD, INC.

Contents

Preface

O
N *GOOD GROUND* by Sister Helen Angela Hurley, published in 1951, brought to life the story of the pioneer Sisters of St. Joseph who preceded us. We learned of their heroism amid the ordinariness of their lives and admired their courage in answering a call in 1851 to serve in the new diocese of St. Paul in the Minnesota Territory. They gave us the example of loving one another and those with whom they worked. They showed their love by forming community and by ministering to others through education, health care, and social service.

On Good Ground satisfied our desire to know more about our roots in St. Paul as we commemorated our centennial. Now, as we celebrate the 150th anniversary of the St. Paul Province, we present *Eyes Open on a World: The Challenges of Change* to share with others the story of the renewal that has taken place in the past fifty years.

Recently those interested in women's place in history have turned their attention to women's religious congregations. Many historians are doing research and writing on congregations of women religious. Some formed an organization, the Conference on the History of Women Religious, in 1988 and through their newsletter inform members about new publications and ongoing research in the field.

Meanwhile many read in the newspapers of the plight of women's religious congregations faced with declining membership; however, another story is emerging as attested to by the Conference on the History of Women Religious. Many congregations have gone through a process of renewal and are experiencing new vitality. Reading such works as this book, scholars will gain important insights into why the experience of women religious merits being treated as an integral part of American history.

Many historians are currently publishing works that treat the experience of women religious as part of the mainstream of American history, most recently the highly readable and well-researched *Spirited Lives: How Nuns Shaped Catholic Culture and American Life, 1836–1920* by Carol Coburn and Sister Martha Smith. In showing Sisters of St. Joseph as pioneer feminists, this book brings out the meaning of religious life for a new generation alert to feminist concerns.

Although *Eyes Open on a World* does not attempt to predict the future, its story of the last half century inspires hope for religious life. Those who support women's quest for equality will be heartened by this story of the response of the Sisters of St. Joseph of Carondelet of the St. Paul Province to the needs of the times and the ongoing call of the gospel. As women of the church we try to live out our charism of unity and reconciliation with God and neighbor and to do "all of which woman is capable" (from an early document of the Sisters of St. Joseph).

Karen M. Kennelly, CSJ

Sister Karen Kennelly, who has a Ph.D. in history from the University of California–Berkeley, is editor of the History of Women Religious Newsletter *and of* American Catholic Women: A Historical Exploration *(1989) and author of many articles.*

Introduction

*E*YES OPEN ON A WORLD: *The Challenges of Change* is part of our celebration of the 150th anniversary of the arrival of the Sisters of St. Joseph in St. Paul in 1851. In telling our story we began with more questions than answers. How has our community been reformed and renewed through the challenges of change? What difference has our presence made in the church and the world? What core values continue to sustain us? How does our story reflect what has happened to other women? How have our eyes been open on the world?

Throughout the book we explore and analyze the changes of the past fifty years and the effects of these changes on our community, the Sisters of St. Joseph of Carondelet of the St. Paul Province. Perhaps no other period in American history has witnessed such tension between the individual and community as has the period from the 1950s to the present. All structures and organizations within society have struggled with these tensions. The Catholic Church and congregations of women and men religious within the church are no exception.

As dedicated women in the church with a recognizable heritage and spirit, we have always shared the common mission of serving God and neighbor. As our province community faced the tensions of change, we differed among ourselves about the ways of addressing external and internal changes. Obstacles to change came from many sides: from structures in our religious community bound by a Constitution and long-standing traditions, from the hierarchical structures of the church, and from the moral, economic, and political thought in our nation and our world.

In the 1950s we were identified by our religious garb and by the works we had undertaken: teaching, health care, and other works of justice and mercy. Our local religious communities were organized around the ministries of the sisters living there. Designated superiors had immediate authority over our lives. As women religious we adhered strictly to canon (church) law because hierarchical legalism prevailed in church affairs. We were considered daughters of the church, in a subservient position to the clergy yet set apart from the laity. Like all women religious at that time we waited for directives from those in authority. Thus, when Pope Pius XII in the early 1950s called women and men religious to adapt to modern times, we responded. The Sister Formation Movement, the Second Vatican Council, and societal movements regarding civil rights, feminism, and Vietnam War protests in the 1960s challenged us further. *Eyes Open on a World* tells the story of our response as individuals and as a community to a changing world.

This book is a collaborative effort in every sense of that word. Our province leadership team, Sisters Margaret Belanger, Margaret Kvasnicka, and Ann Walton, supported a proposal from Sister Mary E. Kraft, then communications director and archivist, in 1996 to explore the possibility of a publication that would update previous written accounts of province history. All agreed it was important to update the 1951 publication of *On Good Ground* by Sister Helen Angela Hurley because of the revolutionary changes that have occurred in the past fifty years. Conversation in brainstorming sessions and among two committees focused on the same questions over and over: What kind of history should this be? What process should we use? What should be the tone of the book? Who will be the audience?

We wanted to provide an account of these years and hoped to suggest that our community has a future that we embrace with enthusiasm. We insisted that the account be honest and show the struggle and diversity within the community. Our goal was to strive for balance and honesty in reflecting on issues that challenged our community and individuals immersed in these issues.

The first committee, known as the Core Committee (Sisters Clare Blanchette, Vera Chester, Roseann Giguere, Karen Kennelly, Mary E. Kraft, Joan Mitchell, John Christine Wolkerstorfer, and consociate Carmen Johnson) invited members of the province community interested in this project to meet for a sharing of ideas. Sisters and consociates were invited to submit proposals, and later that same invitation was extended to former members of the province. The Core Committee identified tentative themes that have come to focus the book: reaching out, letting go, coping with change, and looking ahead.

A second committee, which came to be called the Editorial Committee (Sisters Alberta Huber, Mary E. Kraft, Eleanor Lincoln, Catherine Litecky, and Jean Wincek, joined later by Sister Ansgar Holmberg as illustrator and artistic adviser), began to organize the book. This committee invited all interested community members for further conversation to help shape the book. Gradually the Editorial Committee identified topics and potential contributors. During several meetings with the larger group of contributors we clarified working assumptions that have guided the book's development. We also determined sections and chapters and identified focus questions for contributors.

After discussion involving the Editorial Committee and the contributors, this basic message began to emerge: We, the community of the Sisters of St. Joseph, as women active in the church and in society, have been influenced by movements of change in church and society over the last fifty years. In turn, we have led, influenced, and brought about significant change. The rediscovery of our historical roots has been fundamental to our responding to needs of the times and to effecting change.

Writers, working in groups, prepared chapter manuscripts based on lived experience, interviews, and research in the province and congregation archives. In December 1999 the contributors presented their manuscripts to Laura Beaudoin, who had been hired as editor. She then collated this material into a first draft of the entire book.

As the Editorial Committee reviewed this draft, the need for consistency of information and a common voice to tell our story became apparent. Through a series of six manuscript drafts, during which the original contributors twice were invited to review revised chapters, we had the manuscript ready for publication in December 2000.

Approximately sixty-five sisters, consociates, and former members were involved, in one way or another, in preparing the book. Both the contributors and a number of reviewers, both inside and outside the community, gave us feedback. We value their suggestions, many of which were incorporated into later drafts. From the beginning *Eyes Open on a World* has been a collaborative community process benefiting from the gifts of individuals while drawing on the strength and wisdom of the group. The task of preparing this book reflects how we work in almost every sphere of our lives. We function collaboratively with team leadership, with open committees, and with volunteers for planning our many activities.

From the vast amount of detailed material submitted by the contributors, the Editorial Committee was challenged to know what information should or should not be included. Each sister in the province has a story and deserves to be named, and we wish we could have mentioned each one, but we had to set page limits. The stories we chose illustrate how our community has been reformed and renewed through change.

Our collaboration includes many individuals and groups to whom we owe much gratitude.

We are grateful for all the Sisters of St. Joseph, past and present, who have lived the story we tell.

We are grateful for the many colleagues who have collaborated with us in our ministries or supported them by generous gifts of time and financial support.

We are grateful for the bishops and archbishops of the Archdiocese of St. Paul and Minneapolis who have maintained open and friendly relationships with us during the past fifty years. In particular we acknowledge our current archbishop, Harry Flynn, for his pastoral and loving concern for us as a community and our retired archbishop, John Roach, who has inspired us with his efforts on behalf of justice and ecumenism, as well as his support of women in the church.

We are grateful for the many priests, other clergy, and women and men religious who have worked with us over the years in a variety of projects and ministries.

We are grateful for all those who have been part of our lives: our families, friends, former community members, and, of course, the countless students, patients, clients, and all others who have given meaning to our lives.

In addition to the contributors and reviewers listed in the back of this book, we gratefully acknowledge others for their encouragement, support, and helpful suggestions. We are especially grateful to the province leadership team of 1994–1999 and the current leadership team of 1999–2004 (Sisters Christine Ludwig, Susan Oeffling, and Dolore Rochon), who entrusted us with the task of preparing this book.

We acknowledge Ann Thompson, energetic and expert facilitator, who guided our early meetings and helped us to arrive at a working plan for our task. Laura Beaudoin, our editor, has served her "novitiate" in working with us. She has been unfailingly wise, patient, understanding, and competent. She probably now knows more about us than we know about ourselves! We are more grateful to her than words can express.

The Editorial Committee
Alberta Huber, CSJ
Mary E. Kraft, CSJ
Eleanor Lincoln, CSJ
Catherine Litecky, CSJ
Jean Wincek, CSJ

The Feast of St. Joseph
March 19, 2001

"Eyes Open"

1

Reflecting on Our Roots

A S A GROUP OF US ARRIVED at the Cathedral of St. Paul to celebrate the centenary of the arrival of the first four Sisters of St. Joseph, one sister said, "If the weather was as bad as this in 1851, I would have taken the next boat back to St. Louis." History tells us that the weather was indeed blustery, but those new arrivals stayed—and that is why we were singing and praying at a eucharistic liturgy in the cathedral on November 3, 1951, to commemorate the arrival of the Sisters of St. Joseph in Minnesota Territory. As they stepped off the riverboat, those first brave sisters faced the unknown in a strange place, a frontier town.

Certainly they had no idea of how their small beginnings would develop during the century and a half that lay ahead. Nor could the hundreds of us, singing with gusto there in the cathedral on November 3, 1951, have imagined the changes the next fifty years would bring by the time of our sesquicentennial celebration in 2001.

At that time, in 1951, we looked back with great interest to the stories of our first century in Minnesota. Sister Helen Angela Hurley had chronicled these years in her well-researched history, *On Good Ground: The Story of the Sisters of St. Joseph in St. Paul.* She traced our story from its simple beginnings to the variety of ministries in which we were serving by the time of our centenary year: 17,224 pupils in our grade

schools and 2,430 students in our ten high schools in Minnesota and North Dakota, 938 students enrolled at the College
of St. Catherine, plus five hospitals and several nursing
schools, and two orphanages. Noting that there was "a good
deal of misunderstanding of convent life" (p. 270), Sister Helen
Angela let her readers inside the convent walls.

Looking back now from the perspective of 2001 we have a
long history to remember. Our story did not begin in 1851; it
actually began in France in 1650. From that time we have been
guided by a mission and spirit of love and service to church and
society. This mission has carried us from Le Puy-en-Velay, a
small village in southern France, in the mid-seventeenth century; to Lyons, France, in the years immediately after the French
Revolution; and to countries on other continents, including the
United States in 1836 and then the Minnesota Territory in 1851.
In our journey through time and place we have been enlivened
and encouraged by the spirit of our early sisters.

We have always liked to retell our history. But our knowledge and appreciation of our early sisters in France have been
expanded and enhanced since a research team of ten Sisters of St.
Joseph, fluent in French, went to Le Puy, France, in 1969 to study
our origins. The team included a St. Paul sister, Sister Mary Henry
Nachtsheim, professor of French at the College of St. Catherine.
The team had been formed in response to directives from Rome
and from the Second Vatican Council, which encouraged religious
congregations to search out their roots. The research team was
commissioned by the U.S. Federation of the Sisters of St. Joseph,
formed in 1966, which currently represents twenty-two separate
congregations. Through the meticulous work of the team we
learned much about our early history and spirit.

The research team built upon the work of historian Father
Marius Nepper, a twentieth-century French Jesuit who devoted
his later years to research on the origins of the Sisters of St.

Joseph and the life of his fellow Jesuit, Father Jean-Pierre Medaille. Father Medaille is considered the founder of the Sisters of St. Joseph along with the first six sisters. Together the research team and Father Nepper published in translation the several documents Father Medaille had prepared for the first Sisters of St. Joseph, including the original *Constitutions for the Little Congregation of the Sisters of St. Joseph.* More than three centuries later Father Nepper wrote *Origins: The Sisters of Saint Joseph*, translated from *Aux Origines des Filles de Saint-Joseph* by the research team in Le Puy.

Father Nepper characterized the Sisters of St. Joseph from his perspective in his poem, "Portrait of a Daughter of St. Joseph." Recently Sister Susan Hames of the St. Paul Province has set to music his words: "Eyes open on a world . . . , ears attentive . . . , spirit alert . . . , sleeves rolled up for ministry . . . , in continual joy of spirit."

After intensive and extensive study of the origins of the Sisters of St. Joseph, the research team gave contemporary expression to the spirituality of the sisters in a consensus statement, which continues to shape us as a community. In part it reads:

> Stimulated by the Holy Spirit of Love
> and receptive to the Spirit's inspirations,
> the Sister of St. Joseph moves always toward
> profound love of God
> and love of neighbor without distinction
> from whom she does not separate herself
> and for whom, in the following of Christ,
> she works to achieve unity
> both of neighbor with neighbor
> and neighbor with God
> directly in this apostolate and
> indirectly through works of charity.

Where did this spirituality come from? We can trace it back to our first sisters who formed a community in 1650. We know the names of the first six sisters who gathered in Le Puy-en-Velay: Francoise Eyraud, Clauda Chastel, Marguerite Burdier, Anna Chalayer, Anna Vey, and Anna Brun. These women were uneducated but dedicated to God's service. Only one, Marguerite Burdier, could read and write. Although she did not make religious vows, she served as mistress of novices.

With the inspiration of the preaching of Father Medaille and his encouragement, these six women dedicated themselves to a life of prayer and of service to those who were poor and needy at a time when people suffered greatly from the effects of war, plague, and corruption in church and state. Because at that time the church gave approval only to cloistered communities of women religious, the need was great for active religious women to combat poverty, ignorance, and heresy.

By dividing the city of Le Puy among them in order to find those people most in need of their attention, the six women cared for the sick and orphaned. They also taught lace making to impoverished young women so they would have a way of supporting themselves other than by prostitution. Without cloister or habit the sisters were respected for who they were. As they moved among the people of Le Puy, they dressed in the widow's garb of the day so they would be, as most of us are in 2001, indistinguishable from other women.

In one of the original documents, the "Little Design," Father Medaille described the hopes of this new community named for St. Joseph. The Daughters of St. Joseph, as they were then called, were a remarkable departure from other religious communities of the time. The sisters immersed themselves in every good work "of which woman is capable." In the documents he prepared for the sisters, Father Medaille was in effect synthesizing what he found their spirituality to be, combined with what he was preaching to the laity throughout southern France. The sisters' prayer, which was to be both personal and communal, reached outward through the corporal and spiritual works of mercy. Unity and ongoing reconciliation formed the heart of this gospel-oriented spirituality, which always sought the balance of love of God and love of neighbor. Not only did each sister aim to live always in union with God and with others, but her mission meant that she worked to achieve the unity of neighbor with neighbor and of neighbor with God. This "great virtue," the love of God and all else, was the "good news" of what, in Father Medaille's words, was to be named the "congregation of the great love of God" because God's love always called and sustained the Daughters of St. Joseph.

Not long after the little community had gathered around the kitchen fireplace of their first home in Le Puy, Father Medaille left the sisters to continue his apostolic preaching

elsewhere in France. Meanwhile, new communities of Sisters of St. Joseph developed and spread throughout the country. They evolved into distinct congregations and were only vaguely aware in those early days of their common origins.

The restored kitchen in Le Puy as it was in 1650, where our first sisters sat before the hearth to pray and share their lives with one another.

By the time of the French Revolution the sisters had established over 150 communities in eighteen dioceses of France. During the French Revolution the sisters were scattered, most to their own homes. Authorities imprisoned many of them, and five were guillotined. The death of the tyrant Robespierre saved some sisters by allowing them to escape the guillotine at the last minute. Mother St. John Fontbonne was one of these. She gathered together a number of communities, some formerly Sisters of St. Joseph, into one Congregation of the Sisters of St. Joseph with Lyons, France, as its center. At the time of her death in 1843 the Lyons congregation had 244 houses and 3,000 sisters in and beyond France.

Through Mother St. John's initiative the mission to America in 1836 became the first overseas expansion of the Sisters of St. Joseph, who eventually came to have members on six continents. They were encouraged, and their journey funded, through the generosity and missionary zeal of Countess de la Rochejacquelin, who sold her jewels to secure the funds. She, like many laywomen before and after her time, allied herself with the sisters' mission to serve; she especially wanted the sisters

Our sisters standing near the guillotine toward the end of the French Revolution, as painted in 1918 by Sister St. Luke Kelly. (Used with permission of the Sisters of St. Joseph of Philadelphia.)

to teach Indian children. Six young sisters, including two of Mother St. John's nieces, set sail to New Orleans and then up the Mississippi River to Carondelet, a village near St. Louis. Bishop Joseph Rosati of the extensive St. Louis Diocese had invited the sisters to educate deaf children. The need for health care, social services, and education was so great that the sisters, at the invitation of other bishops, soon set out for other parts of the country, much of it still mission territory. The sisters showed sensitivity to the needs of immigrants, who were arriving in large numbers. A number of American-born women joined the Sisters of St. Joseph, and the communities the sisters established continued to grow and spread in the United States.

In 1851, fifteen years after Sisters of St. Joseph had landed on American soil, the new bishop of the Minnesota Territory, Bishop Joseph Cretin, invited the sisters to his vast diocese to teach the Indian and white children. Four sisters traveled up the Mississippi by riverboat and arrived at the village of St. Paul on an inclement night in November. They were taken to the diocese's "block" on Bench Street between Cedar and Minnesota Streets. These sisters, two of whom were American-born, formed the first mission of the Sisters of St. Joseph in Minnesota. Mother St. John Fournier from France, who was the leader of the little group, had earlier established a community of Sisters of St. Joseph in Philadelphia.

Sister Francis Joseph Ivory, the youngest and most enthusiastic of the four with a taste for adventure, later wrote a vivid memoir of those early days: "We then were shown Our New home a small fram[e] shanty on the Riverbank. We took our first meal, Supper, (Nov. 3) in the vestry of the Old log Church. We had difficulty to get Water enough to make our tea as there was but one Well in the town and that was locked up" (Hurley, p. 25).

Mother St. John Fournier described it this way: "[O]ur room served for oratory, refectory, community room, parlor and dormitory. At night, we put our mattresses, two on the table . .*. and two on the floor. We opened school in the old church near us" (Hurley, p. 27). According to the letters sent back to Carondelet, a few days later they opened a school that was to become St. Joseph's Academy. They used as a classroom the vestry of the log cabin church, which was the site of the first Cathedral of St. Paul. Later the school was moved from the vestry into the church proper.

Meanwhile the community adage, to do "all of which woman is capable," was called forth. When a cholera epidemic broke out in St. Paul in 1853, the sisters, who had come to teach, found themselves nursing the cholera victims in the log cabin church hastily converted into a makeshift hospital. In 1852 Bishop Cretin had begun planning for a hospital, which

Here in one log cabin on the banks of the Mississippi River in St. Paul, where sisters came in 1851, was the first Cathedral of St. Paul and the beginnings of St. Joseph's Academy and St. Joseph's Hospital.

in 1853 was under construction but not yet ready. So the same log cabin church that had seen the beginnings of St. Joseph's Academy in 1851 was the initial site of St. Joseph's Hospital.

Bishop Cretin's appeal to the Society for the Propagation of the Faith brought the sum of 37,500 francs ($7,500 at that time) to the St. Paul mission. This contribution made possible not only the sisters' school and the hospital but also an orphanage and a school for the Indians. In *On Good Ground* Sister Helen Angela Hurley tells the story of the Indian mission in Long Prairie and many more stories of our first 100 years in St. Paul. Through expansion of membership we were able to spread our ministries beyond St. Paul and Minneapolis to rural Minnesota, Wisconsin, and the Dakotas.

The relatively simple lifestyle of the early sisters gave way to more regimentation and standardization in our daily schedule and customs. Some of this regimentation was imposed upon us by the revision of canon law in 1917. By 1951 we were spending between two and three hours daily in community prayer and always took a companion when we left the convent. In prayer and schedule, our community life had come to resemble that of cloistered orders.

Nevertheless, we expended much effort on our active ministries of education, health care, and social service—such as caring for orphans, visiting prisoners, and feeding the hungry. Involvement in social justice, liturgical renewal, and women's education began early in our history in Minnesota, a seedbed for political and church activity, and we have continued to be actively involved. The St. Paul Province was blessed by community and church leaders who promoted these values. Notable were Sister Seraphine Ireland and her famous brother, Archbishop John Ireland, whose family came from Ireland to St. Paul shortly after the sisters arrived in 1851. John Ireland became one of the earliest seminarians for the young diocese of St. Paul. Ellen (Sister Seraphine) Ireland, along with her sister Eliza (Sister St. John) Ireland and their cousin Ellen (Sister Celestine) Howard, attended the new St. Joseph's Academy and were among the first women to join the Sisters of St. Joseph in St. Paul.

Sister Helen Angela Hurley notes that these women "were not born superiors any more than [John Ireland] was born an archbishop" but that they were "persons of purpose and ability in their own right" (p. 216). They all exercised leadership in the St. Paul civic and religious communities. Archbishop Ireland contributed much to the Americanization of the Catholic Church—contributions for which he has been acclaimed by many and criticized by some. "He looked on the sisters as an integral part of his Americanizing process" (p. 217), Sister Helen Angela affirms, especially through their influence in the Catholic schools.

For the St. Paul Province, Mother Seraphine provided leadership beginning with her administrative positions in a number of schools, as well as at the St. Paul Girls' Orphanage. When she was forty, she began her long career as provincial superior and served in that role from 1882 until 1921, an unprecedented thirty-nine years. Archbishop Ireland's con-

Community leaders in the early history of the province: Mother Seraphine Ireland (right) *with her sister, Mother St. John Ireland* (left), *and their cousin, Mother Celestine Howard* (center).

fidence in his sister undoubtedly encouraged her in the establishment of six hospitals, two orphan asylums, an infant home, forty-five parochial grade schools, fifteen high schools, and a college.

Mother Seraphine and her brother had discussed the founding of a college for women, and as early as the 1880s she had selected a site. Despite skepticism in St. Paul and elsewhere about higher education for women, the College of St. Catherine was opened in early 1905.

In the first 100 years since our arrival in St. Paul, and in the fifty years since that time, we have valued our heritage stemming from Le Puy and are still growing in our awareness of it. Phrases from our earliest lore and written documents, which so interested the research team of sisters, motivate us. "Divide the city," a phrase describing the plan of action of the first Sisters of St. Joseph in 1650, reminds us today to see the needs around us. The phrase "dear neighbor" tells us, as it told those first sisters, that everyone is a neighbor close to our hearts and to God's love. Always mindful of the dear neighbor, we are called, as were those first sisters, to engage in all works "of which woman is capable." Nowadays that includes just about everything. We, like them, are called to "be of one heart" and to "have one spirit."

We keep reminding ourselves of this early spirit. So did Jean Houston, a world-renowned speaker, at a conference of the Federation of the Sisters of St. Joseph in Philadelphia in 1995. She told the assembly that the Sisters of St. Joseph were "on a roll." After reading our early documents, which the conference planners had sent to her, she described our heritage in contemporary terms. Houston, a writer, philosopher, and teacher who believes in the possibility of realizing the fullness of human potential, noted that the early sisters had found "a new manner of living in the midst of the upheavals of the seventeenth century." She regards them, and us today, as "lead-

Forum International Saint-Joseph brought together more than 1,200 Sisters of St. Joseph from around the world to Le Puy and Lyons, France, in 1993. Here sisters from Madagascar present offertory gifts in the cathedral at Lyons.

ing-edge thinkers" who are "ahead of much of the world" by being "grounded in spirit with a passion for the possible." Referring to the terminology of our earliest documents, she said the increasingly complex world of today needs "a small design in a big world." Houston, senior adviser in human development for the United Nations, believes the Sisters of St. Joseph have a "genius for bringing many cultures together." Expanding on the "dear neighbor" concept, she challenged those assembled to serve in a new universe by having a new mind for all the complexity and chaos of "planetary civilization." Quite a challenge for all of us as we prepared at that time for the twenty-first century.

Equally challenging are the words of one of our newest members, who hopes to make her first profession of vows in 2001, the year of the sesquicentennial celebration of the St.

Paul Province. She sees a similarity between the first women—
"so few of them"—and current new members. "Those first
women in France had no idea of what the Sisters of St. Joseph
would become or how their work would be built upon." This
new member sees current sisters, like those early sisters, as
"creative problem solvers" who recognize the precariousness of
our time and culture and respond to the needs of the people.
She surmises that if Francoise Eyraud, one of the early leaders
in seventeenth-century Le Puy, or Mother St. John Fontbonne,
who refounded the Sisters of St. Joseph in nineteenth-century
Lyons, or the pioneer sisters in the Minnesota Territory were to
visit the St. Paul Province in the third millennium, they would
find women who would remind them of themselves. "They
might be surprised at the large numbers of sisters and at the
variety of ministries but would recognize common values and
the same spirit. They would be pleased."

The words of both of these women can encourage and
challenge us as we look back at our 350-year history, especially at the fifty years since 1951. These years brought great
changes in our lifestyle and ministries as well as in the world
around us, but we hope the spirit of the Sisters of St. Joseph
will continue to sustain us as we try to meet the changes ahead
in both church and society.

2

Moving Toward Renewal in Church and Community

S ISTER MARY MARK MAHONEY remembers that one Sunday years ago, when she was teaching at St. Michael's School in Grand Forks, North Dakota, a youngster saw the sisters waiting outside the parish church and shouted, "Here comes the church!" Other children elsewhere also knew that the sisters somehow represented the church and called us "church ladies." A middle-aged woman speaking recently of her childhood experience said, "The sisters made us feel that the church was our home."

Through our association with countless children and adults over the years, we have tried to help shape their knowledge and understanding of the church. This knowledge and understanding shifted dramatically in the 1960s when the bishops at the Second Vatican Council undertook the renewal of the theology of the church. Saintly Pope John XXIII called over 2,500 bishops and theologians to Rome from all over the world to begin the tremendous task of what he named *aggiornamento,* or updating of the church. He hoped their work would bring fresh air into a church needing to open its windows to the world.

The Council touched us personally even before its official beginnings when Archbishop William Brady of the Archdiocese of St. Paul and Minneapolis died in Rome on October 1, 1961, while attending a preparatory session. Our community, to which his sister, Sister Mary William Brady, belongs, mourned the loss of a great and gifted American church leader.

A majority of us in our community and in the church welcomed the dynamic process of change set in motion by the decisions of the bishops at the Council. On the other hand, critics of some of the changes complained that not only windows blew open but doors as well. Both the excitement and turbulence in the church as a result of the Council deeply affected us and other communities of women religious. At the time of the Council many of our communities were already involved in renewing our lives and in trying to return to the spirit of our founders. We engaged in personal soul-searching and faced the challenge of changing relationships with the church, especially with the hierarchy.

As Sisters of St. Joseph we had a model in Teresa of Avila, a Spanish mystic and reformer of religious communities in the years following the Council of Trent, held in the sixteenth century to respond to the Protestant Reformers. On her feast day, October 15, we celebrate the tradition of our founding as a community in 1650. Like saints and prophets before and after her, Teresa heard God's call to reform and renew her own congregation and the church of her day. She struggled to make her theological views known at a time when women were forbidden to do so. In spite of her difficulties with some church authorities, she regarded herself as a "daughter of the church." Many of us today who admire her efforts at renewal prefer to use the term "women religious in the church" to describe ourselves.

How did the theology of the church change as a result of the Second Vatican Council? When we Catholics reflected on the church before the Council, we thought primarily of an institutional, hierarchical model symbolized by a pyramid. In this model of the church the pope stood at the top, bishops and clergy ranked beneath him, and the laity formed the broad base. Women religious belonged with the laity. By contrast, the Council bishops introduced other models of church in which the concept of *collegiality,* or shared responsibility, for decision making began to be used not only among bishops but also at diocesan and parish levels.

Archdiocesan leaders returning from the Council began to put collegiality into practice by establishing a pastoral council in 1972 to advise on archdiocesan affairs. The first council of twenty-four members in our archdiocese included Sister Rosalie Ryan of the College of St. Catherine's theology department. Our sisters in the St. Paul Province have continued to influence the local church in significant ways. Many sisters since the Second Vatican Council have served on a wide variety of commissions, such as those concerning urban affairs, ministry, ecumenism, worship, and women. Recently Sister John Christine Wolkerstorfer, professor emerita of history at the College of St. Catherine, wrote *"You Shall Be My People": A History of the Archdiocese of St. Paul and Minneapolis* in celebration of the sesquicentennial of the archdiocese.

Archbishop John Roach established one of the first diocesan commissions on women in 1979. We were involved from the beginning—Sister Catherine McNamee served as its first chair, and the commission hired Sister Margaret Kvasnicka as executive secretary. The St. Paul Province furnished an office in our Administration Center for the commission.

Reflecting on the role of women's leadership in *The Catholic Spirit,* retired Archbishop Roach writes that for real leadership in the church, women's voices need to be heard. He states that in the past, church leaders did not take advantage of women's leadership potential. To ignore the creative gifts of women, Archbishop Roach says, is "ignoring a treasure." Thanks to countless women (including many of our sisters in the Archdiocese of St. Paul and Minneapolis), he says, the church has become more responsive to God's call for a just and good society.

An appropriate symbol for a model of the church using collegiality in decision making would be concentric circles at whose center is Jesus Christ. The most important document on the theology of the church emerging from the Second Vatican Council, *Lumen Gentium*, emphasizes the central role of Jesus Christ. The document begins, "Christ is the light of all nations."

No one image or model can adequately describe the church. Because the church is a mystery, the bishops used scriptural and poetic language to describe it as they sought to renew the theology of the church. Two biblical images used in the Council documents are the "People of God on pilgrimage" and the "church as the Body of Christ." These images had great appeal to us as we engaged in our renewal process. The idea of pilgrimage encouraged us as we endured the hardships and uncertainties of renewal; it gave us a sense of purpose and even joy. As we rediscovered our founding spirit of promoting the love of God and of neighbor in order to achieve unity and reconciliation, we could resonate with the model of church as the Body of Christ.

We had, in fact, begun our pilgrimage of renewal even before the Council met. It has come as a surprise to many of us to learn that the beginnings of our renewal process came from our response to directives issued by Pope Pius XII. In 1950 at the First General Congress of the States of Perfection, he urged communities of women religious to adapt religious life to better serve the people of God. He suggested that we return to the spirit, or *charism*, of the founders of our religious congregations.

Pope Pius XII asked leaders of religious congregations to establish a new national organization fostering collaboration as a way of furthering the work of the church in the United States.

Two years after the first gathering in Rome he again stressed the need for religious communities to work together and to update aspects of religious life that interfered with meeting the needs of contemporary life. Such obstacles included oppressive rules and regulations that stressed uniformity and detail, archaic clothing, and even the class distinctions that existed in some communities.

Among the leaders of religious congregations, Sister Eucharista Galvin of St. Paul, at the time the superior general of the Congregation of the Sisters of St. Joseph of Carondelet, played a significant role in establishing in 1956 a national organization for collaboration. Known for her visionary leadership and gentle humility, Sister Eucharista had served as professor of history, president of the College of St. Catherine, and provincial superior of the St. Paul Province prior to her selection as superior general of the congregation. The new organization, named the Conference of Major Superiors of Women, had legal status as a church body and, according to church law, was accountable to Vatican authorities.

Sister Eucharista Galvin went to Japan to teach English after completing her ministry as superior general of the Congregation of the Sisters of St. Joseph of Carondelet.

In the first decade of its existence our congregational leaders as members of the conference focused on the spiritual welfare of American sisters and on increasing their effectiveness in ministry. When the members changed the name of this organization from the Conference of Major Superiors of Women (CMSW) to the Leadership Conference of Women Religious (LCWR), Vatican officials delayed the approval of the name change for three years, perhaps because they regarded it as presenting a new view of religious life.

At the conclusion of the Second Vatican Council, the LCWR expanded its initiatives not only to include internal issues but also to implement theological changes promoted by the Council. Two theological teachings in particular revitalized religious life: the first, that all persons are called to holiness, and the second, that holiness is to be achieved in this world. The universal call to holiness proclaimed in the document *Lumen Gentium* moved away from the concept of religious life as an exclusive state of perfection. The document states that the measure of a person's love of God and love of neighbor determines the holiness of each individual, rather than the person's state of life or vocation. Not only is holiness based on love but also on immersion in the world for the sake of mission. The Council recognized that the church is for the world and its mission is in the world. Holiness is to be achieved in the world, not apart from it. Concern for the good of all humanity and for the needs of the world, the document reminds us, is the responsibility of every Christian.

Before the Second Vatican Council, farsighted members and leaders of our congregation and others had set in motion plans for the renewal of religious life. We entered early into this renewal, which involved radical changes in community life. Clergy and lay Catholics were accustomed to thinking of us as withdrawn from the world and living in large convents, wearing long black habits and veils, and working in church institutions. They began to see us involving ourselves in social and political issues, living in small groups in neighborhood housing, wearing contemporary clothes, and working at jobs outside of church institutions. Some of us who had been teachers now began experimental new ministries such as literacy centers for immigrants and homes for women and children in need.

Our desire to engage in new ministries coincided with the determination of religious communities like ours to enable young sisters to complete college degrees before assigning them to teaching, nursing, or other work. The Sister Formation Movement, a new pattern of educational preparation for ministry combining personal, intellectual, and spiritual growth, began in the mid-1950s.

We in the St. Paul Province were blessed in having the faculty, staff, and administrators of the College of St. Catherine interested in furthering the movement's goal of integrating

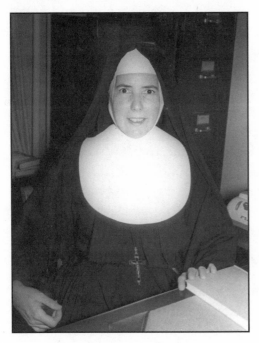

sound spirituality with personal and professional competence. Sister Annette Walters of the St. Paul Province, who had been professor of psychology and academic dean at the College of St. Catherine, played a major role in this

Sister Annette Walters, pictured here in 1966, played a major role in achieving the Sister Formation Movement's goal of integrating sound spirituality with personal and professional competence.

movement. As executive director of the Sister Formation Conference from 1961 to 1964, she worked diligently to improve the quality of life of all sisters. Sister Annette brought to her position a brilliant mind, a deep commitment to social justice, and a desire to integrate faith and competence in sisters preparing for lives of service in the church and the world.

Many of our young sisters in the province did not know Sister Annette personally, but all were familiar with her as their instructor in a video course she developed on human psychology, which was part of their juniorate studies. The juniorate was a postnovitiate period of training devoted to intellectual, spiritual, personal, and professional development. In the St. Paul Province the juniorate continued from 1955 to 1968. One sister remembers her two years in the program "as a wonderful, exciting time in which the whole world was opening up to us." Another remarked how much she appreciated the juniorate experience for "the high value placed on the development of the whole person and on the integration of the academic and spiritual." A third sister spoke of how grateful she was to begin teaching knowing how well prepared she was for her assignment.

Not only young sisters beginning their lives of service but also many other sisters benefited from Sister Formation Conference programs, such as Sister Formation Summer Institutes and other workshops. We had opportunities for theological updating and growth in awareness of current ideas in scripture and liturgy, as well as in the psychology and sociology of religious life. We came to realize that professional competence is an act of justice in every ministry.

The Sister Formation Conference also urged our communities to provide opportunities for graduate study. The St. Paul Province already had a long tradition of assigning sisters to graduate study to continue the availability of well-educated sisters for the College of St. Catherine, our hospitals, our grade schools and high schools, and our other institutions.

With more young sisters studying in the juniorate program, fewer sisters were available to teach in parochial schools. In 1955 Sister Eucharista Galvin, our superior general, wrote a letter to the mother provincials of each province telling them that she had already spoken to some bishops about the Sister Formation Movement and had received their approval. She urged the provincials to speak to their local bishops and concluded her letter, "I am sure they [diocesan authorities] also will be cooperative and make the necessary sacrifice to meet their needs until we can supply teachers to them."

The "necessary sacrifice" meant, among other things, pastors having to hire lay teachers for parish schools at salaries considerably higher than the stipends paid to sisters. Parishioners had, of course, to supply the money. During this time, an increasing number of sisters became interested in working directly with people living in poverty. Other attrition came as our community, like others, experienced a large decline in vowed membership.

Yet, through the influence of the theological teachings of the Second Vatican Council, our province's continuing participation in the renewal efforts of the Leadership Conference of Women Religious, the lasting effects of the Sister Formation Movement, and a sense of solidarity with the U.S. Federation of the Sisters of St. Joseph, we felt a new interdependence among women religious in the United States.

The Federation continues to identify itself in its charter as "a dynamic union of Sisters of St. Joseph which moves us to a greater consciousness of our kinship of grace and calls us to fidelity to that grace." The twenty-two congregations of the Federation continue to cooperate in various research projects such as the 1995 Collaborative Viability Study, of which our congregation was a part. Together with the other members of our congregation we gathered data to answer the question of whether our congregation showed promise of survival. Project leaders hoped the data would help religious communities assess their strengths, identify challenges, seek assistance where appropriate, and plan for the future. All congregations of the Federation agreed to share one another's findings.

Our province found that the areas of leadership and membership generated the most interest and showed greatest diversity of opinion. We challenged our leaders to continue to invite participation in decision making, to maintain good communication, and to incorporate changes as needed. The study pointed out the importance of examining how we have embraced or denied diversity among members. It also showed our economic stability as a strength, and as a result we have

More than 1,550 sisters representing the congregations that make up the U.S. Federation of the Sisters of St. Joseph stand at the base of the St. Louis Arch in June 2000. At this Jubilee celebration of the 350th year of the beginnings of the Sisters of St. Joseph, the sisters rallied for justice, especially to erase violence and dismantle racism.

been able to share our resources with others in need, including congregations belonging to the Federation.

We find that it is in celebrations with the sisters of the Federation that we feel our solidarity as Sisters of St. Joseph. At the events sponsored by the Federation we realize most clearly that our province is only a small part of a much greater whole. This became evident to us when in 1995 we gathered with more than 1,200 Sisters of St. Joseph in Philadelphia to celebrate the theme "Little Design in a Big World: A Grace That Sustains." Many from our province participated in that event and also in the June 2000 Federation national event, "Sound the Trumpet"—a call to jubilee held in St. Louis, Missouri, to celebrate the 350th anniversary of the founding of the Sisters of St. Joseph. In reflecting once again on our roots we joined 1,550 women representing the over 10,000 members of the Sisters of St. Joseph in North America. In prayer, in demonstrations for social justice concerns, and in discussions we responded enthusiastically to our role as sisters in the church. While we rejoiced in our gains in striving for equality of women in the church, we recognized how much more needs to be accomplished.

3

Relating to Our Carondelet Congregation

A S SISTERS OF ST. JOSEPH of the St. Paul Province we have created new forms of governance to carry us through changing views of ourselves as women in a religious community. Our ways of governing ourselves have been influenced by our geographic location in the populist Midwest, by our relationship with the church, especially our local church, and by our context within our religious congregation, the Sisters of St. Joseph of Carondelet. How we govern ourselves and how we relate to our Carondelet congregation have evolved along with the many other changes we have experienced in our personal and communal lives in the past half century.

The movement from the top-down authority of the 1950s to today's broad-based community governance continues to reflect how we see ourselves individually and as a province. We have moved from focusing on details of daily life and a hierarchical emphasis to subsidiarity and relational governance. We value open sessions for decision making and operate within the framework of pluralism and diversity rather than of uniformity.

One way to view the evolving story of our governance is through tracing the relationship of the St. Paul Province to our congregation, the Sisters of St. Joseph of Carondelet. This governmental structure was formed from the early communities of Sisters of St. Joseph that had spread out from the village near

St. Louis called Carondelet in the mid-nineteenth century. Although the original six sisters who came to the United States were immigrants, the community quickly became American-ized. As early as the 1850s Sister Celestine Pommerel, the superior of the community in St. Louis (Carondelet), began plans for a central governmental structure for the sisters in the United States that would make the American community inde-pendent of France. The plan included developing regional provinces that would operate independently but with some connection to the motherhouse in St. Louis.

The complexities involved in establishing a centralized government in the United States included the difficulty of com-munication and travel between the United States and France, the rapid Americanization of the community, and clarifying lines of authority. In communities in France, the local bishop had final authority, but many Sisters of St. Joseph in the United States wanted papal approval, which would limit the power and control of the local bishop and allow the community to make its own decisions. The new congregation would allow the sisters to elect one of their own as superior general, who would reside in St. Louis and serve as the central authority. Each regional province, however, would have the authority to accept and edu-cate novices and to operate its own institutions.

Sister Celestine's death in 1857 delayed the plan for restructuring, but in 1860 the sisters came together to affirm their support for the idea of central government. After long and emotional discussions and ultimatums from the bishops of dio-ceses where the sisters were serving, only those communities centered in St. Louis, Albany (New York), and St. Paul became provinces of the general congregation. In 1900 Los Angeles became a fourth province, and in 1922 the vice province in Georgia joined the St. Louis Province. Also in the twentieth cen-tury sisters from the various provinces of the congregation went to missions in Hawaii, Japan, and Peru, which later became vice provinces, and to a mission in Chile.

Final papal approval, granted in 1877, promoted the independence of the newly structured congregation, gave the sisters some assurance of autonomy, and freed them from the control of local bishops. But this autonomy from diocesan control was not without other problems of authority. In the early 1900s, papal approval brought more interference, this time from Rome, requiring religious congregations to standardize their internal organization, impose partial cloister, and restrict sisters' travel.

These standards were actually contrary to our founding spirit. The code of canon law in 1917 imposed further regulations, limiting the autonomy and flexibility of women religious. Superiors became responsible for "reporting" to Rome regularly about adherence to the regulations. This tightening of control demanded that sisters of all congregations align their constitutions with canon law. As a result, the Sisters of St. Joseph of Carondelet, who had traveled and worked independently, were now significantly curtailed in their activities.

Nevertheless we carried on with our lives in our provinces and within our congregation. The provincial superiors met every six years with the superior general in a congregational chapter. At these congregational chapters, the provincial superiors discussed issues that affected life and ministry in the provinces, which gave the superior general the opportunity to connect with the sisters. Later, elected delegates from each province expanded the scope of the chapters. Despite the uniform regulations imposed by Rome, the provinces, as well as the congregation as a whole, continued to be shaped by their own identities and unique qualities.

The congregational chapters act as the highest authority in the congregation and the provincial chapters as the highest authority in a province. Provincial chapters always meet prior to the congregational chapters, and their main task is to prepare for the congregational chapter. In these chapter sessions we discuss issues we are facing in the province and in the congregation and consider their impact on our common life and ministry.

The history of both congregational and provincial chapters over the past fifty years shows growing openness on the part of the congregation and the provinces. For the St. Paul Province our chapters have both given shape to and reflected our lives as women religious.

The first provincial chapters in the congregation took place in 1959. At the convening of the first provincial chapter in the St. Paul Province we found hints of changes to come. At the congregational chapter held the next year, these changes gave us new freedom and moved us toward greater respect for individual differences and needs. Some of us began to drive cars; we were allowed to go to movies and listen to radios to a limited degree; and principals of schools could have private phones in the convents. Chapter delegates in 1966 involved themselves in heated, and sometimes amusing, discussions of the religious habit and made suggestions for modifying it by shortening skirts and wearing color-coordinated veils. The restrictions on sisters' lives that, since the early 1900s, had curtailed our activities began to lessen. We could now say our prayers in English, with prayer times adapted to the needs of each individual sister or each local house. We could do spiritual reading privately instead of in a group.

The congregational chapter of 1966 advocated the development of new expressions of spirituality by encouraging each local community to develop communal prayer forms in addition to or in place of lauds and vespers, the official morning and evening prayers of the church. Subsequent chapters also addressed the issue of apostolic spirituality, which stood in contrast to semi-monastic spirituality. It was becoming clear to us that we should reemphasize the apostolic spirituality of our first sisters.

Because of the call of Pope Pius XII and of the Second Vatican Council for religious communities to rediscover their roots and study their origins, the provincial and congregational chapters beginning in the mid-1960s moved toward a deeper understanding of our lives as women religious. For the first time, the delegates distinguished between issues that were specifically provincial and those to be forwarded to the congregational chapter. One such issue promoted at the Council was the principle of *subsidiarity*, which directs that a decision be made by those most immediately affected by and responsible for carrying out that decision. Subsidiarity became a foundation for our future discussions and decisions. The provincial chapter applied this principle in determining a more "democratic" way of selecting leaders. We began the practice of voting for our province director and for local superiors instead of having them appointed, as had been the earlier practice.

This philosophical shift moved us closer to our charism as Sisters of St. Joseph, with the focus on us as individuals living our lives as members of a community. It is in our local communities that we share our joys and sorrows, thereby renewing our energies for service to and with our neighbors.

At a later provincial chapter we put into practice the principle of subsidiarity. One of the sisters serving in Peru asked the support of the St. Paul Province in obtaining representation for the sisters in Peru at the congregational chapter. As a result of this request the St. Paul provincial chapter members elected a sister from Peru as one of St. Paul's delegates to the congregational chapter.

St. Paul delegates at that chapter also recommended that, for both the province government plan and for the con-

Sisters from across the United States who served as delegates to the congregational chapter of 1966 held in St. Louis. The following year Sisters of St. Joseph began to wear contemporary dress.

gregation's Constitution and Complementary Document, the description of the local community be placed *before* the description of congregational government in order to move away from the hierarchical order of placing general government first. This philosophical shift had great significance in how we viewed authority.

The work of the congregational chapter of 1966 was to revise the Constitution in light of the Second Vatican Council. Much of the preparatory work concerned the vows of poverty, chastity, and obedience in particular and community life in general. The issues to be addressed at this congregational chapter were too numerous to be covered, so another chapter was convened in 1969.

In order to broaden our thinking, this chapter opened itself to experts outside the community and, more importantly, invited sisters who were not elected delegates to attend the chapter for two days. This broadening set the stage for future open chapters and assemblies at which nondelegate observers had voice.

With the emphasis on internal community matters decreasing since the late 1960s, congregational and provincial chapters shifted to a more global view. Our mission of justice came to the forefront. Throughout the 1980s and 1990s, the Acts of Chapter, our congregational chapter decisions, called for commitment to "right relationships" with those people who are economically exploited and impoverished as well as a commitment to understand global systems that perpetuate cycles of injustice. These Acts of Chapters also urged action, in collaboration with other groups, to promote the fullness of life, including sustainable food production, a healthy environment, and access to education, health care, housing, and employment.

This renewal of our mission of justice goes back at least to the congregational chapter of 1969, when we began to set up structures to facilitate the work of justice. Chapter members mandated the formation of congregational and provincial working groups, including one for social action. Since that time groups have addressed strategies for urban change, relief of poverty, investment and corporate responsibility, education on citizen involvement, racial justice, and world peace. These groups helped us focus more effectively on the role of women religious in promoting justice and social change, and they called us to a renewed emphasis on our promotion of gospel values.

Looking at justice issues from a global perspective prompted us to examine our understanding of diversity within our community. The superior general and her council commissioned a team of sisters representing each province to undertake a congregation-wide study to be entitled "Pluralism, Diversity, and Unity in the Sisters of St. Joseph of Carondelet." According to the study, unity grows when we respect diversity. Thus diversity rather than uniformity in our community was a way to unity. The study concluded that pluralism and diversity can strengthen unity. The results of this study supported us as we made changes in many aspects of our lives in community.

As we moved in the direction of pluralism we became more concerned about individual rights everywhere. In 1978 another team of sisters from throughout the congregation reflected on how the operative values of the socioeconomic systems of the developed world relate to global injustices. Sisters became increasingly involved in civic and political arenas, and all of us grew in our concern for human rights, poverty, oppression, world peace, and the environment.

Our province responded to the *Economic Pastoral Letter* issued by the bishops of the United States and reaffirmed the need for our involvement with ministries directly affecting social structures that impact economic systems. Because ministry is the expression of who we are, a deeper understanding of our call to ministry has always been one of our concerns at provincial and congregational chapters.

In a similar way membership and the vowed life are topics we regularly discuss. The congregational chapter of 1978 recommended a study of membership issues, including the possibility of temporary membership. Interest in exploring ongoing commitment as an alternative to permanent vowed membership grew in the 1970s and 1980s. Ongoing commitment would mean that a member would annually renew her vows rather than make permanent commitment. After intense discussion by various groups we decided that membership meant growing into community and that members would continue to make permanent, not temporary, profession. However, the matter of temporary membership continues to surface from time to time.

Each province has its own membership plan, subject to approval by the congregational chapter. Our St. Paul plan uses a modification of the Ritual of Christian Initiation of Adults (RICA) for initiating new members, both those preparing for sister membership and for consociate membership, a form of membership developed in the 1980s for persons desiring to associate with us more closely. These internal matters continue to be discussed at congregational and provincial chapters, but more and more our concerns expand beyond ourselves as we focus on justice issues.

In the Acts of Chapter of the congregational chapter of 1997 we reaffirmed "our choice to be in right relationship with people who are economically exploited and impoverished, especially women and children." We also reaffirmed "our need to be in right relationship with earth." We committed ourselves to deepen our understanding of global issues and systemic change and to embrace multicultural realities. We also turned once again to the importance of membership and our own spirituality. In the St. Paul Province we have given attention to the ideas that came to us from the 1997 chapter, focusing on them in personal prayer, in discussion, at our province rituals, and in our ministries.

Since the time when St. Paul became a province in 1860, our relationship with the congregation has brought us many benefits, but being a part of a larger whole has not been without its conflicts. Disagreements and tensions surface occasionally. In one instance, congregational leadership determined that regional superiors should be appointed for each province. These superiors would have authority over sisters in specific geographic regions. Because the St. Paul Province is much more geographically centralized than the other provinces and because we were developing models of relational governance at that time, we decided that we did not need regional superiors. We therefore did not follow the directives of the congregational leaders.

In another situation, the superior general interfered with the right of the St. Paul Province to elect a province director from a slate of candidates nominated by province members. When the superior general questioned one nominee's fitness for leadership, this nominee's name was eliminated from the slate.

In protest, several sisters of the province refused to accept copies of the newly published Constitution of the Sisters of St. Joseph from the hands of the superior general at the ceremony where she distributed the copies.

Despite some tensions our province cooperates in congregational matters. We participated in the study known as "Relationships for Mission," initiated by the congregational chapter of 1993. This study examined the feasibility and desirability of congregational restructuring of provinces. It had been 120 years since the Sisters of St. Joseph of Carondelet received approval to be a general congregation with separate provinces (and later vice provinces and a mission). Some chapter delegates thought the time had come to examine whether this governance structure supported our life and work as we moved into the twenty-first century.

The report to the congregational chapter four years later explained the process and outcome of the study and reaffimed "our intention to remain one congregation with autonomous provinces and vice provinces" (Relationship for Mission: Final Report—Recommendations to 1997 Congregational Chapter). The study revealed our congregation-wide intent to reverence and respect the variety of cultures within our midst and surfaced our desire for deeper and expanded connections as members of one congregation.

Thus has the relationship between the St. Paul Province and the congregation continued unbroken. We now relate, however, to a congregational leadership team rather than a superior general. Members of our province have served in various capacities in congregational leadership, and we have been involved in congregational study groups, task forces, commissions, and secretariats. Although the St. Paul Province, like other provinces, enjoys autonomy, we have been enriched and strengthened by interrelating with our sisters in other provinces and vice provinces and with those in congregational leadership. We think with one mind about matters of justice. We continue to resonate with the vision and images of the latest congregational chapter in its call: *The well is deep . . . the water living*. The Acts of Chapter invite us to drink deeply at this well through concern for global issues and systemic change, multicultural realities, membership, and spirituality. We look forward to exploring how we can deepen our commitment to action on these issues at our congregational chapter in July 2001: "Called Forth by the Dear Neighbor."

The well is deep . . . the water living, *written in the three languages of the congregation, accompanied the logo for the congregational chapter of 1997 of the Sisters of St. Joseph of Carondelet.*

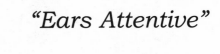

"Ears Attentive"

4

Changing Province Governance

TODAY, WHEN AN ENVELOPE ARRIVING in the mail contains the agenda for a meeting of the Province Assembly, the policy-making body of the St. Paul Province, we do not experience this as an earth-shaking event in our lives. But fifty years ago, the idea that a policy-making Province Assembly could even exist would have been cause for great excitement. It is doubtful that even the most radical thinker among us then would have imagined that one day we would make decisions about the future direction of our province, ministry, and common life, or that the persons presiding over the group would be members of a leadership team we selected ourselves.

But all this did happen, not, however, as an isolated phenomenon but as part of major changes in religious life. In the past fifty years a transformation has taken place in the governance of the Sisters of St. Joseph of Carondelet. We have moved from being a congregation and province based on a centuries-old hierarchical model, in which authority moved from the top down, to one in which sisters share power in collaborative, participative ways.

How our province got to where we are today is in itself a story of collaborative participation. The process of change in governance that began with the development of the Delegate Assembly in the late 1960s, and then of the Province Assembly thirty years later, took place in a widespread environment of change and was helped along by many groups and individuals. Among them were, most importantly, the sisters themselves, along with expert consultants and our province leadership.

When we began the task of redesigning the governance of our province, we had only the models of civil forms of government, but renewal movements in the church and in religious life beginning in the 1950s supported our efforts. Our questions were: Did our existing modes of governance meet the needs of the sisters? Practically speaking, what kind of structures did we need and how should they operate?

The process of resolving these issues was complicated, because those of us trying to resolve them were ourselves complicated. As human beings we had been formed by many experiences and influences. Some of those experiences we had in common, like growing up in a country that had familiarized us with both the theory and practice of democracy. The changes in the church were cause for both hope and pain for us as well as the rest of the laity. The Vietnam War and the Watergate Scandal impacted us just as they did the rest of the United States. These events left a distrust of government and its leaders, as well as suspicion of authority.

Our personal experiences also affected us, including family life, sibling and peer relationships, education, and the age at which we entered the congregation. Experiences in religious life had left some sisters with painful memories of how they had been treated by individuals in authority or of inequities in common life. Some had found religious life repressive rather than life-giving.

But we had a lot going for us. Our province had stressed the importance of education by preparing sisters for their work, and we were considered to be highly professional and competent in our ministries of health care and education. In hospitals, in schools, and in our religious community sisters held management and leadership roles. Sisters were specialists in theology, philosophy, political science, and sociology—all very useful fields of expertise for our present needs. As a group of highly educated women, we had been trained to think, to be creative problem solvers, and to be open to new ideas. Over the years, many of those in authority had made serious efforts to ground us deeply in the spirit of religious life. Geographically, a large number of us lived and worked in Minnesota, a populist state where the influence of grassroots opinion shaped public policy. Geographic closeness made frequent personal contact easy as we tried to gather the best ideas from the largest possible number of members.

We saw ourselves as a group of women who voluntarily joined our lives for a common goal. We shared a belief that the Spirit speaks not only through individuals appointed as superiors but also through both the individual member and the group as a whole. Governance, we decided, is the framework from which and through which community life and ministry should function.

Over the years, a few changes were made in the original governance plan drawn up in 1967, and in 2000 we adopted a plan that broadened the membership base of the assembly, but we have never departed from our grassroots approach. We aimed to design structures that would safeguard, benefit, and enable both the individual and the group; so in writing our plan we reversed the order in which the three divisions of governance were traditionally delineated and began with a description of the local level instead of with the provincial superior. At first, many members of the other provinces considered this change revolutionary, but eventually they agreed that this reversed order emphasizes the principle of subsidiarity. When our Constitution was updated in 1984, it, too, used the same format by acknowledging that it is in our local communities that we live out our daily commitments, practice Jesus' command to love one another, and, by consensus, make appropriate decisions. For example, all of us in a given community house are responsible for determining the local budget and making wise expenditures in keeping with our religious vow of poverty.

Planning the Delegate Assembly brought out our creativity. Since our province membership was too large to make direct democracy feasible, we agreed that this policy-making group had to be representative. The major decisions involved the number of members and how to choose them.

Size was the easier of the two issues to settle, although no one was sure that the number we settled on, thirty-six, was workable and would provide adequate representation. The basis for choosing delegates was a thornier matter. Would representatives be elected by ministries, by age categories, by interest groups, or simply at-large? Opinion finally settled on at-large elections, but there were many reservations. How could we be confident that minority opinions would have a voice? To address this concern, we adopted the idea of forums. Sisters with similar interests, ideas, and/or objectives could organize a forum of at least twenty members; and since whoever chaired it also served as a member of the Delegate Assembly, minority opinions and special interests could be assured of a voice and vote.

Our provincial superior at the time, Sister Mary Edward Healy, opened the first meeting of the Delegate Assembly in 1968. The first official action of the members was to choose a presiding officer. In imitation of civil government, we were attempting to separate legislative and executive powers, but this proved to be both impractical and contrary to church law. The provincial superior continued to preside over meetings. Eventually, we also included each sister in a province-level leadership position as an *ex officio* member with the result that communication improved and our work became more collaborative.

Though widespread support existed for the new governance format, a tendency toward polarization posed an undeniable threat. Other religious congregations experienced the same problem and some actually divided into separate communities. How did we avoid this fate? Part of the answer might lie in the existence of the Delegate Assembly and the forums. They provided us with an outlet for disagreement; through one mechanism or another, all had a chance to be heard. Most of us were firmly convinced that division was not the answer. Another reason was the character and governance style of our first elected province director, Sister Genevieve (Miriam Joseph) Cummings. As presiding officer of the Delegate Assembly, Sister Genevieve was a skillful parliamentarian who insisted on fairness and on respecting the rights of all members. As province director she was a peacemaker and an attentive listener. Her calm composure inspired confidence and helped smooth over difficult situations.

Becoming accustomed to new structures and procedures takes time, and as the years passed, the need for revision became evident. The impetus for changes in structure began to take shape in the 1970s as province members addressed the idea of team leadership. During that same decade, we explored the decision-making process of group *discernment*, which means opening to the Holy Spirit's action within the group through prayer and in dialog with others to determine a decision.

Our province's use of boards broadens the base of decision making. In the early days, most decisions were made by the provincial superior. In broadening the base of authority, we have put many of those decisions in the hands of sisters who sit on community boards. These boards are not included in our plan of governance but are established when needed. Requests from sisters for cars, for study, for travel, or for engaging in new ministries are directed to the appropriate board. The leadership team and/or the Delegate Assembly has been involved in establishing or staffing these boards. What is important is that the system works remarkably well and exemplifies relational governance.

Our changing view of major leadership roles is illustrated by the titles we used over the years to designate persons in these positions. The change from provincial superior with one assistant to a province director with eventually two assistants, support staff, and numerous boards reflected a move to share authority. The present term, *leadership team*, denotes an equal sharing of the leadership authority and responsibility among three sisters. The three agree on the area for which each will

Sisters Susan Oeffling, Ann Walton, and Margaret Belanger became the first leadership team in the St. Paul Province. They were chosen by a community discernment process in 1991. As a team, they shared authority and responsibility for province leadership during their term.

take responsibility. One member of the team selected in 1999 points out that the system works because each person brings a different background and experience to community situations. "Three heads and hearts are better than one," she says.

Sisters who hold the major leadership positions really wear two hats. Besides having responsibilities that relate to the religious and canonical nature of the community, they are also administrators of the province as a civil entity. According to church law, certain decisions concerning finance and membership cannot be delegated by the leadership team. In finance, the team has sole responsibility for, as church terminology puts it, the alienation (selling) of province property. The team is also responsible for all matters of membership, especially admitting candidates. In the areas of both finance and membership, the team can and does call on others for advice and expertise when appropriate. For example, the province council and treasurer, the vice president for administration, and the Province Assembly, with its finance committee, are the team's chief financial advisors. They assist in duties such as preparing the annual budget, monitoring investments, and making retirement fund decisions.

One factor influencing us to change to team leadership was the feminist theological movement. Feminist theologian Elisabeth Schussler Fiorenza speaks of the church as a "discipleship of equals." Theologian Letty Russell writes of a "household of freedom." Women's presence and voice were being uncovered in Scripture scholarship, spirituality, and church history. Since many of us were engaged in exploring these new understandings of women in the church, it seemed imperative that our governance structures reflect the movement from hierarchical structures to relationships of equality and participation.

The transition to team leadership in the early 1990s was not without tension. The new team chosen in 1991 struggled to

develop both a working, practical model and an understanding
of the concept of a team. Gradually we became accustomed to
the new idea. In subsequent province selection processes in
1994 and 1999, there was little questioning of the team model
of leadership and, by 1999, there was greater comfort and sat-
isfaction with discernment as the process for selecting leadership. We had moved from the appointment of leaders, to
province members voting, to discernment. No process has ever
satisfied everyone. The members of the province council were
chosen by the leadership team and affirmed by the Delegate
Assembly. Together, team and council serve as the civil and
canonical authority of the province.

While the idea of team leadership was still in its infancy,
there gradually emerged a questioning of the structure of the
Delegate Assembly. Our membership had declined from 1,230
in 1967 to 407 in late 2000. Some sisters began to wonder if

*The province community blesses and sends forth the 1999 leadership nomi-
nees. After a week spent together in prayer and discernment, the sixteen nom-
inees unanimously chose three persons to be the new leadership team.*

we still needed a representational policy-making group. Could we possibly devise a structure and system that would allow everyone to participate and vote as a committee of the whole?

Without question the Delegate Assembly served us well as a vehicle for representative participation in our governance. But as other changes occurred in our lives, it became clear that the growing desire for an enhanced role for all members in province decision making demanded a change. The time had come to extend the principle of subsidiarity to its next logical step by replacing the representative style of governance of the Delegate Assembly with a new assembly in which all province members have voice and the preferred decision-making method is by consensus. And so the Province Assembly came into existence in May 2000. Now we not only share our community life and pooled resources but also share the power of common decision making.

Launching this new venture in relational governance is both exciting and challenging. Over the past fifty years a deepening understanding of the principles of religious governance has enriched our lives. The Province Assembly enables us to live out these principles more fully. By providing an arena for respectful discussion where listening goes much deeper than merely hearing words, we draw on the wisdom and talents of all members. In the Province Assembly, all members are equal. We discern and work together collaboratively, striving for consensus.

Can we succeed in doing all of this? The motto of the St. Paul Province is *Possumus*—"We can." A structure only creates possibilities. We understand that for this new plan to succeed a sense of ownership and personal responsibility, which includes a generous willingness to be informed and involved, is absolutely essential. Since our members have already demonstrated these qualities during the process that produced the final form of the Province Assembly plan, we feel our expectations are justified.

5

Reimagining Religious Life

I N MANY WAYS THE STORY of each Sister of St. Joseph in the St. Paul Province in the past fifty years *is* the story of the province. Our individual decisions have shaped what the province has become and have given direction to our future. Profound convictions about community, ministry, faith, and spirituality have sustained us in the past decades and have allowed us to reimagine religious life.

In the late 1950s, we still lived a "cloistered" life and carried on active ministries. Spiritual values and a common horarium (schedule) bound us together: rising, morning meditation, prayer and Mass, breakfast, work, afternoon recreation, prayer, dinner, evening recreation, prayer, and retiring. This routine was fairly consistent from convent to convent, with accommodations made for sisters working in hospitals and at the College of St. Catherine.

We all wore the same religious habit and were called "Sister." We were rarely seen in public outside of the schools and hospitals in which we served. Whenever we were outside the convent, we had a sister-companion. Sisters assigned to domestic duties or laywomen managed our kitchens and cooked our meals. The convent had parlors set aside for visits with family and other laypersons. There was a sense among us of "that's the way it has been and the way it will always be."

As novices in 1957, Sister Mary Lois Sweeney (left) *and former member Sister Mary Christopher Cermak baked hundreds of chocolate chip cookies for the community. Sister Mary Lois has continued working in the ministry of food service for over forty years. She along with a number of other sisters involved in domestic ministry provide a valuable dimension to community life.*

Some visionary sisters among us, however, recognized the need to make changes in our personal lives for the sake of our mental and physical well-being. Known for her advanced thinking in psychology, Sister Annette Walters in the early 1950s planned and organized mental health workshops for the leaders of various religious communities in the United States. Encouraged by the success of these workshops, Sister Annette brought her concern for mental and physical health to the Sister Formation Conference.

Another visionary woman, Sister Bertha Poupore, provincial superior in the mid-1950s, showed her compassion and understanding not only for our immediate needs but for long-range community needs. In 1954 she opened both our retirement home and a vacation home. Sister Bertha was aware of the increasing number of older sisters who were living in convents intended for sisters in active ministry. To remedy this situation, she established Bethany Convent, designed to meet the physical, social, and spiritual needs of retired sisters. Each resident had a private room and half bath. Sister Bertha insisted that the rooms be as large as possible for individuals but small enough so the rooms could never be turned into doubles. From the beginning the sisters at Bethany have shared the responsibility to create an atmosphere supportive of personal and communal growth and love. Bethany is known throughout the community, and beyond, for its warm hospitality and for being a "powerhouse" of prayer.

Sister Bertha also believed sisters needed yearly vacations, so she arranged for the purchase of an old lodge, called Timberlee, on Big Fish Lake, about eighty-five miles north of the Twin Cities. When we started using Timberlee, our superiors relaxed a few community rules so we could enjoy our lake

Sister Bertha Poupore lived at Bethany Convent for some years before she died in 1985. The card distributed at her funeral contained scriptural words that reflect her loving spirit: "My sisters, love one another as I have loved you." Many times over the years we have remembered Sister Bertha and blessed her for her foresight. (© 2000 STAR TRI-BUNE/Minneapolis–St. Paul)

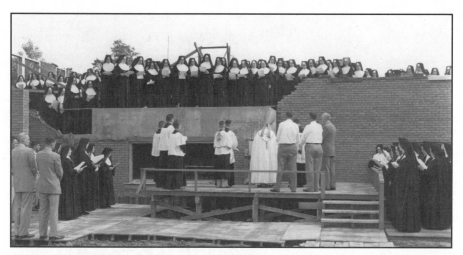

Sisters assemble in 1953 for the dedication of Bethany Convent. For nearly fifty years, sisters have enjoyed the excellent care provided there by our sisters and many lay health care professionals.

vacations. We still had to wear our habits at all times, except when we were actually swimming in the lake. One of the rigid regulations stated that a rope had to connect the boat to the dock at all times, allowing us to go out only a hundred feet into the lake. This rule was established because a sister in another community was said to have drowned, weighed down by her habit. However, ingenuity and creative use of more rope enhanced our boating pleasure and led to the elimination of this rule.

As the years passed, life at Timberlee became freer. We sat in the lodge with our feet up before the roaring fire in the huge stone fireplace, sunned on the dock or swam around it, dived off the raft, fished from one of the boats, and hiked in the woods and around the lake. While at Timberlee we were not required to observe the rule of silence, so we talked and talked! We came to know one another in new ways. Often the conversation turned to ways we could change or even reform the community.

Timberlee is a place for relaxation, conversation, and reflection. This photo was taken in 1963, a few years before renewal affected our mode of dress.

In this 1979 photo, women exploring the possibility of sister membership take time to enjoy the natural beauty of Timberlee.

Sometimes arguing, sometimes agreeing, and often laughing, we shared many ideas that eventually became part of our renewal.

Our time at Timberlee prepared us for, and even precipitated, changes in our lifestyle. The most obvious evidence of our renewal and transformation was our change in dress. The first Sisters of St. Joseph in Le Puy, France, in the 1650s wore widows' garb so they could go out to serve the poor without male chaperones. Their head covering and long sleeves and skirt made them inconspicuous. But we kept this style of dress for 300 years, and so the black-and-white habit became more and more conspicuous as decades passed. The movement to alter the habit began with our experimenting with a few contemporary styles of black, brown, blue, and white street-length dresses with veils. In our first attempts at modification we assumed we would adopt one standard dress. That notion rapidly fell away, and soon sisters wore clothing styles that made them indistinguishable from laywomen.

Sisters who changed their manner of dress thought they were heeding the call to "not separate themselves from the dear neighbor," but those who chose to retain the habit worried about the erosion of the clear boundaries and roles the habit afforded. We experienced many years of internal tension around this polarity of thought. The issue of the habit and its meaning in the context of religious life helped us develop a model for working through profound chasms of difference within our community. The deep commitments we had made to the core values of our community and to the vowed life allowed us to persist in a dialogue fraught with tension and dissension. Again and again we returned to our shared core values until it became clear that these values rather than clothing were the bonding fabric.

We realized that we needed to live and operate differently in a world that was changing rapidly. The opportunity to exper-

Fourteen sisters gather for a formal photo after the ceremony in which they made their final profession of vows on August 6, 1967. This "reception" was the first group to make final vows wearing the "new" religious garb, modified habits.

iment in our way of living gave us the responsibility of maturing in ministry and community.

An equally powerful current of change occurred with the rediscovery that the Sisters of St. Joseph were established in France to be an active rather than cloistered community. The original documents of the first sisters promoted an active ministry beyond the cloister, which had limited the lives of other women religious. The rediscovery, in the late 1960s, that our charism was to engage actively in the corporal and spiritual works of mercy, to live in small groups, and to work among our neighbors, resulted in an extraordinary release of energy to serve in a wide variety of new ministries.

Many societal and community stressors began to collide about the same time. We were examining our identities and our ministries. Some sisters, with others in society, questioned everything. The Civil Rights movement and the Vietnam War signaled an era of protest, and some of us learned the skills of peaceful protesting, community organizing, and political caucusing. For some sisters, change was occurring far too fast; for others, change wasn't happening fast enough. Still others of us faced questions we had never asked before. We began to explore a new sense of being women with choices. Living like the rest of society gave us access to new relationships, awakening in some the desire for a sexual intimacy that had been foreclosed at a relatively young age.

Members began to leave the community, first in a trickle, then in a stream, and then in what seemed like a flood. One person called it a hemorrhage of youth, energy, talent, and leadership. Within the space of about five years the province lost over 250 of our 1,200 members. Those who remained experienced deep sadness because of the rupture of relationships that had been forged over many years. Those of us who stayed found ourselves in an extended period of grief and loss, followed by doubt, self-examination, and recommitment. For our community it was a time of questioning whether our mission and charism were still compelling. As a community we lost confidence and had less passion for encouraging women to share our calling.

Many of us began to explore career options that suited our personal strengths and inclinations as well as our convictions to work for justice and equity in the broader society. Some of us welcomed the opportunity to move into ministries in direct service to those who are poor or disenfranchised; as a result some of us left the schools and hospitals, which had been the only venues for ministry until the late 1960s. This led

to a mounting crisis. The institutions that relied on the sub-
sistence-level stipends of the sisters to balance their budgets
now had to hire lay employees for considerably more money.
Hospitals and schools faced sales, closings, or mergers. In an
effort to stabilize the resulting volatile education crisis in the
Archdiocese of St. Paul and Minneapolis, the school superintendent devised a merger plan for neighboring parish schools.
Some pastors resisted the plan, and some sisters chose to
remain in the schools that did not merge.

These decisions became another source of tension and
division within the community. Some supervisors and principals felt betrayed. Those of us who elected to pursue alternative ministries felt that we bore responsibility for radical
changes. Those of us who remained in the schools and hospitals saw leadership positions go to lay personnel and felt the
strain to maintain our community's mission and vision in these
institutions with fewer and fewer sisters.

Some of us who found that living in large groups of twelve
to fifty did not support our personal and spiritual growth
moved to smaller communities of four, five, or six. We lived in
neighborhoods, attended parish churches, and got more in
touch with the daily lives of those people we worked among.
Since the late 1970s, we have lived in a variety of configura-
tions ranging from living alone in apartments to small houses
of two to five sisters to convents of as many as fifty sisters.

Events in the world around us deeply impacted life in the
community during the 1960s and 1970s. The media brought
images of the Civil Rights movement and the Vietnam War into
our homes daily. Intense discourse among civic, legislative, and
church leaders grew more vehement. Society was in the throes
of deconstructing its mores and beliefs.

What was happening in our community paralleled what
was happening in society at large. We were finding our own

voices and articulating strongly held convictions. The tools and skills of the external protest movements came home to the community in our daily interactions. It was in this area—the creation of governance structures that allowed individuals to live authentically according to their deeply held convictions—that we most relied on our core values to hold us together when our disagreements could have torn us apart.

We experienced a need for members to communicate the profound changes we were experiencing. In 1968 we began to write and publish *Beginnings*, an internal newspaper. *Beginnings* gave us a way to communicate with one another and to know how we lived, worked, and thought, not merely in terms of carrying out a superior's directives but as responsible and mature women. The publication chronicled our evolution and helped us to see ourselves as one, even as we struggled to deal with our differences. As we began to move more comfortably into new work and social settings, new experiences became more accessible. We struggled and learned how to accommodate the remarkable human diversity that earlier had been obscured by similarities in dress, daily routine, and customs.

In the light of profound personal and professional changes in the 1970s, many sisters suffered from the distress of work that did not suit them. Our province leadership appointed a personnel director to help them discover ways to live in personally and professionally satisfying ways while being true to the charism of the community.

In 1975 the community established Derham Community with Sister Mary Kessler as director. This residential program for personal growth for women religious was housed in what had been the convent for Derham Hall High School. During the twenty years of its existence the Derham Community staff served approximately 300 women from over eighty religious communities. Women from all over the country learned personal skills never before demanded of them and reinvented their lives. The Derham Community experience accelerated another new trend—that of sisters who became members of our province by transferring from other provinces and from other religious communities.

As we became more aware of ourselves and each other within the community, we saw that other women were also searching for a sense of identity that went deeper than the roles they played. We were not alone. As women of the church, we joined the women's movement and other protest groups and made the voice of the Sisters of St. Joseph of the St. Paul Province heard in the public arena and in the press.

The women's movement of the 1970s was a catalyst for profound change in society and in our community. Women came together in powerful ways to open doors of opportunity for one another. The valuing of women—how we think and learn, how we act out of concern for the web of relationships in which we live—became an intense focus for all women. Women religious had much to contribute to a movement looking for models of women raised to be leaders, of women supporting women, of women whose lives had never been organized around male employers or husbands, of women who valued the intelligence, competence, and strength of other women.

By the 1980s much of the upheaval in the community and for individuals had stabilized. There remained lingering signs of a more hierarchical time in our difficulties in handling conflict directly and actively rather than indirectly and passively. Because we continually returned to our mission of reconciliation—to restore oneness where it has been broken—we were able for the most part to heal many old wounds related to the changes we had accomplished together. We established a Mediation Council of sisters to arbitrate serious differences between individuals. It has been used only a few times. As we discovered that forming community did not always involve living under the same roof, our coming together became more intentional, with frequent large or small, planned or spontaneous gatherings to celebrate holidays, to pray and reflect, to study, and to plan the future together.

We have each made our own decisions about ministry, within some basic province criteria and with our own sense of a need the community could address through our gifts and strengths. In addition to our traditional ministries of education and health care, we involve ourselves in social work, pastoral care, parish administration, spiritual direction, counseling and clinical psychology, and business administration. We are present in shelters for women who are battered, among the homeless, with AIDS patients, and in home health care. Some sisters have launched small nonprofit businesses focused on social justice, human services, health care, spirituality, publishing, and other entrepreneurial endeavors.

A number of compelling observations further caught the attention of our community. We realized that the decisions of individual sisters to become part of other groups that share a similar vision created a new and expanding network of relationships and opportunities for us to continue our mission. The notion of collaboration has turned from a process internal to the community to an outward focus of cooperation with other religious, civic, and national groups. Our outward focus has made us known in a new way to those interested in our work and even in our way of life. We are now welcoming them to join us as sister and consociate members.

6

Becoming Members

A CALL OR VOCATION TO RELIGIOUS LIFE, as to all other ways of life, remains a mystery. A story related by a third-grade teacher illustrates this. She asked her students, "How do you suppose people know if God is calling them to think of marriage, of being single, of being a priest, brother, or sister?" The answers varied from, "You pray a lot," "You're holy," "An angel tells you," to the answer from a little girl who said, "It feels right in your heart."

The latter response is probably the most time-tested. However, in the past fifty years the process of preparing for religious life has changed significantly. Likewise, fifty years ago the questions of what constituted membership and how one became a member of the community had relatively simple, uniform answers.

Today both questions and answers have become more complex as we experience a resurgence of prospective new members. Some may be inquirers at the beginning of the membership process, candidates for vowed or consociate membership, or sisters desiring to transfer from other communities. In a unique situation, a small congregation, the Sisters of St. Joseph of Nazareth-on-the-Lake, Superior, Wisconsin, merged with the St. Paul Province. Questions continually needing resolution include how we define membership and how we prepare prospective members for holy, happy, and healthy lives in community.

Fifty years ago when young women, often right out of high school, desired to become sisters, they came to the novitiate with other women who felt the same call. As postulants they learned the traditions and practices of the Sisters of St. Joseph in a highly structured six-month program. Their black blouses, skirts, capes, and stockings reminded them daily that they had detached themselves from the world. Prayer, study, and household chores filled their days.

During the six months both the community and each postulant tried to determine whether or not she had an authentic vocation to be a Sister of St. Joseph. Adjusting to a disciplined, unfamiliar way of life brought difficulties to everyone. For some who loved to talk, the rule of silence proved hard to keep. The six months served as a "trial run" for all the young women; some realized that this way of life was not for them and left the program after a few weeks or months.

For those who stayed, their daily schedule paralleled that of sisters working in their ministries of education, health care, or social service, although postulants spent more time in classes on Scripture, liturgy, and community life. Many of the young women experienced for the first time the joy of entering into the spirit of the liturgical year.

Postulants and novices in 1961 have fun roller-skating at the back of the novitiate building at 1890 Randolph Avenue in St. Paul.

The provincial superior and her council, after the young women successfully completed the six months as postulants, approved each woman's entrance into the novitiate. On the Feast of St. Joseph, March 19 (and sometimes on other feast days), the postulants, dressed in white bridal gowns, processed to the altar. At this ceremony, the archbishop received their requests to enter the novitiate, and each young woman received the religious habit she had spent so many hours making. For many this was done under the patient instruction of Sister Rita Joseph Roy, a much-loved sister who spent many years helping postulants and novices with their sewing. At the ceremony each postulant received not only the religious habit but a new name symbolizing her desire to "leave the world" in pursuit of holiness. Now the women entered into a very structured program of studies, including preparation classes for the

Postulants dressed in bridal gowns leave the chapel to return as novices wearing the black religious habit of the Sisters of St. Joseph (1959).

vows. In the novitiate, they would spend two years more determining if they were called to religious life through the process of discernment by means of prayer and dialogue.

The prayer life of the novices, like that of the postulants, included daily meditation, Mass, morning and evening prayer, and the rosary recited in common. Also part of each novice's personal devotion was making the stations of the cross each day. Penitential practices, designed to help them lead disciplined lives, were a part of community living. Novices looked forward eagerly to daily times of recreation. They laughed—and cried—often, perhaps more than ever before in their lives. The group, known as a *reception*, developed an identity that lasted throughout their lives. We often ask each other, "Which reception are you in?"

After completion of the novitiate program and acceptance by the provincial superior and council, novices professed religious vows of poverty, chastity, and obedience. Many of the young women making their vows between 1955 and 1968 then became part of the juniorate program located at the Provincial House, which adjoined the novitiate building. However, a few of the sisters already prepared for ministry were assigned to province ministries. Those in the juniorate program continued to live with the sisters in their reception and attended classes at the College of St. Catherine to prepare for future ministries. The choice of ministry was made by the provincial superior and her council according to the aptitudes of each sister and the needs of the community at that time.

After earning their undergraduate degrees, the sisters were assigned to schools or hospitals or to other work for active ministry. Three years later, all sisters with temporary vows returned to the novitiate for six weeks of preparation before professing final vows, when they would consecrate themselves forever to the service of God and others. This practice lasted until the late 1960s, when sisters made final profession in a church or chapel of their choice. The challenge and invitation of living religious vows came daily to live the life of love and service that they desired from the day they had entered the religious community. In ways they could not have known before, a later statement on a Sisters of St. Joseph brochure spoke to their experiences: "A religious person should have three bones—a wishbone for high ideals, a backbone for good resolutions, and a funny bone for ups and downs."

Because so many young women had joined the community in the 1950s and early 1960s, architects were commissioned in the mid-1960s to draft plans for a new novitiate building. Many of us thought it unwise to proceed with this new building because of the renewal beginning in religious life and the ambiguity it was bringing. The decision not to build proved to be a wise one, since the juniorate program in St. Paul ended in 1968, only thirteen years after its inception. By this time, the number of applicants to the novitiate was down significantly, and many young women, as well as some who had served for many years, were leaving religious life. The women who left the community often put their fine educational and spiritual training to good use in the professions and careers they chose. Some continue to associate in various ways with members of the Sisters of St. Joseph community. The strong bonds they established in the novitiate and juniorate and in subsequent years of ministry remain a significant part of their lives.

The renewal of religious life and societal change in the mid-1960s and early 1970s had an impact on the training received by the few young women seeking membership. A new flexible formation program served as a bridge for a few years. Then as now this program allowed for individual living situations and for differences in educational, professional, and per-

sonal backgrounds. The program respected each woman's educational experiences and guided and supported her in discerning present and future goals. When a woman became an affili-
ate she continued her spiritual and professional training. She
had the opportunity to live with a local community of sisters for
at least one year as an associate before moving to the novitiate
stage of preparation. As a novice, she spent another year or two
studying and preparing for her public commitment to God as a
Sister of St. Joseph.

According to Sister Susan Hames, one of the program
directors in the 1970s, being with these women was exciting
and at times exhausting. One of the greatest challenges was
helping older community members, who had had a highly
structured and uniform formation experience, understand the
more flexible program designed for young adults.

*Young women beginning the formation program enjoy the relaxing atmosphere
of Timberlee.*

For a period of nine years no women entered the community as candidates for vowed life. The changing role of women in society and in the church, as well as questions raised, internally and externally, about the viability of religious life contributed to this dearth of applicants. Within our own community, some of us questioned the feasibility of bringing in new members at a time of uncertainty when we were leaving institutions, redefining ourselves, and searching for the meaning of our being together. During the time of decline in sister membership, the consociate movement began to experience significant growth.

At the beginning of the twenty-first century, we see a resurgence of interest in membership in our community. Many people seek meaning in their complex lives by turning to spiritualities and ministries that speak to their desire for a deeper relationship with God in community. They are searching for a community of women to support and encourage them in their longing for God and in being of service to others. We welcome these people who come to the community with personal maturity, professional training, and often years of experience in responsible positions. Each brings a unique life story. One woman's story illustrates this journey.

A woman who made her first temporary religious profession in 2000 came to our community after having worked for years as a nurse. When she began to seek out information about the Sisters of St. Joseph, she found inspiration and spirituality that involved prayer and action. She identified with our community—in our belief that we can make a difference in society, in the church, in global issues, and in our concern for the earth.

After prayerful discernment, she entered a process of inquiry. Sisters invited her to participate in community events, special prayer, and ritual celebrations. She began her formal association with the community as a consociate but before long decided she felt called to be a vowed member.

As a candidate, this woman shared in the common life of prayer and ministry and took advantage of the many opportunities afforded her for spiritual and theological reflection. Province leadership, in getting to know her and her desire to share her life with the Sisters of St. Joseph, received her into the novitiate in a simple ceremony. She was given the title "Sister" but kept her birth name. As a novice, she lived with a local community and participated in its activities, along with her novitiate program of study, prayer, and preparation for vows. Her program involved her in the intercommunity novitiate program, in which women and men exploring membership in area religious communities meet for classes in Scripture and theology and to discuss and pray over issues of common concern or interest.

After completing her novitiate experience, she made religious vows of poverty, chastity, and obedience for a three-year period. As other women have done recently, she created a special profession ritual to celebrate her commitment to God in the religious life with her family, friends, and sisters.

Of late province members have asked whether the novitiate is a place, a process, or an event. Could it be all three? Over the years, the location of the novitiate has changed several times, from St. Joseph's Academy to the large novitiate building at 1890 Randolph Avenue in St. Paul to a variety of smaller places. Novices, sometimes a hundred or more, lived in the novitiate building from 1912 until 1969, when the building became a dormitory for the College of St. Catherine. The shifts in our living situations and ministries are reflected by this Randolph Avenue building, renamed Carondelet Center. Women now seeking vowed membership live in small communities and have a gathering room in Carondelet Center.

Consociate membership has evolved during the past twenty years as we have explored alternative forms of membership. The membership committee of the Delegate Assembly focused its work on developing modes of lay association, and in 1982 it received approval for the resolution that the St. Paul Province establish a program for persons who want to be identified as Sisters of St. Joseph of Carondelet associates. Later the word *associate* was changed to *consociate*.

The word *consociate* comes from the French word meaning *companion*. Consociates, who are also known as associates in other provinces and as *ohana* by our Hawaiian sisters, are women and men of a variety of lifestyles and faiths who find their spirituality, work, and passion for justice in harmony with that of the Sisters of St. Joseph of Carondelet. Consociates do not take the traditional vows of religious life but make a commitment to live the community's vision of "moving always towards a profound love of God and love of neighbor without distinction" within the context of their own lifestyles and responsibilities. They are financially independent of the community.

According to Sister Judith Kavanaugh and other sisters who initiated the consocium, they recognized the need to keep things fluid. They chose not to define the consocium rigidly and not to put strict parameters on this new form of membership.

Since 1982, approximately sixty women and men have made commitments as consociates. In 1987 the renewal of commitment of consociates was

Carmen and Jeff Johnson, both consociate members, at a 1988 community gathering.

added to the March 19 St. Joseph Day liturgy, when the sisters traditionally renew their vows.

The province in 1993 hired a consociate, Shirley Lieberman, as a salaried member of the membership team. Under her leadership we took a major role in establishing a regional network of directors of consociate/associate programs and of encouraging collaboration at the national, congregational, and Federation levels. A few sisters disapprove of the inclusion of consociates as members because they think consociates blur membership boundaries. However, most of us, consociates and sisters alike, feel a sense of belonging through a common charism, passion for justice, and willingness to be a part of one another's life journey.

These connections create positive energy that comes from shared experience. Consociates plan and participate in rituals, prayer services, and liturgies and take advantage of personal enrichment opportunities. Some work with or volunteer in province ministries, such as Sisters Care, Peace House, or Bethany Convent. Consociates participate in community meetings and work on committees such as the membership committee and the Justice Commission. Since 1991 the leadership team has invited a consociate to act as a consultant to the provincial council.

The St. Paul Province has been further blessed and enriched by the transfer of a number of women religious from other communities. These women have asked to become members for a variety of reasons, especially that of compatibility of their own spirituality and ministry with our charism and work. Recently support groups of sisters have begun to help sisters who are transferring become more familiar with how we live as Sisters of St. Joseph. After the canonical process of transfer is complete, the sister makes a formal transfer of her vows in a ceremony at which she is officially welcomed.

In one instance, the Sisters of St. Joseph of Nazareth-on-the-Lake in Superior, Wisconsin, a small diocesan congregation, requested a merger with us in 1985. After going through a long and difficult process of prayer and discernment, the "Superior sisters," as they came to be known, joined us as a group, although three sisters chose to join other congregations of Sisters of St. Joseph. They had served the diocese of Superior for almost eighty years. Like a number of other small communities in the United States with limited resources, they had considered the possibility of merging with a larger community as an alternative to dying out as a congregation.

Sister Ursula Schwalen, president of the Superior congregation at the time of the merger, has spoken of and written the history of her community and of the personal sorrow the

twenty-eight sisters felt over the decision to leave their home. In the article "Looking Back That Others Might Look Forward," in *Review for Religious*, Sister Ursula describes the process and the legal technicalities involved in achieving a merger. She also speaks of the emotions that each sister

Sister Ursula Schwalen published Called . . . and Re-Called to Serve, *a history of the Congregation of the Sisters of St. Joseph of Nazareth-on-the-Lake, Superior, Wisconsin.*

faced in the decision to leave the familiar for the unknown. What helped in the transition, she notes, was the warmth, love, and concern with which the St. Paul sisters welcomed them. Some of the elderly, retired sisters came directly to Bethany Convent, while others continued their work in an active ministry.

Today, Sister Ursula recalls the experience by saying, "Thanks be to the St. Paul CSJs for sharing their home with their 'distant cousins' from Superior, Wisconsin. We have been blessed with a stable, pleasant, and wonderful home [Bethany] in which we can spend the remaining years of our life in continuing the mission of the gospel."

We do not know what new forms of religious life will emerge in the decades ahead. We hope that future members, when asked why they are choosing to become members of the Sisters of St. Joseph, will respond, "It feels right in my heart."

"Spirit Alert"

7

Living Out Our Religious Vows

NOT FOR OURSELVES BUT for those who come after us." The words of Sister Annette Walters, quoting Susan B. Anthony, set the theme for the first Symposium on Vowed Life sponsored in 1998 by the St. Paul Province for Sisters of St. Joseph from across the United States and Canada. The congregational chapter of 1997 had commissioned such a dialogue to focus on three questions: What gives life to, or what dilutes, the mission of the congregation? Is the expression of our commitment through the vows of poverty, chastity, and obedience life giving for mission, or is it in need of rewording or reimaging? What are the implications of our commitment for the people of God?

The gathering was in part a memorial for Sister Annette on the twentieth anniversary of her death. As the printed program said about her, "She was a sister and friend, psychologist and professor at the College of St. Catherine, author, human rights advocate and activist, feminist, and . . . futurist." All of the discussion reflected the spirit of this prophetic woman.

Sister Katherine McLaughlin, one of the prime movers of the event, said afterward in an article in *Together* (November 1998, p. 10), the province newsletter: "In the past forty years we have radically transformed our perceptions of poverty, chastity, and obedience. We have gone from an understanding rooted in canonical language to a theologically reflective contemporary

Sister Toni Nash of the Los Angeles Province shares a conversation with participants at the 1998 Symposium on Vowed Life. She is pictured here with Sisters Karen Hilgers (left) *and Catherine Steffens, both of the St. Paul Province.*

understanding which suggests that we make one gift of ourselves, and that gift spins itself out in three dimensions of our lives. Do we need to change the vows? No. Do we need to live the vows uniformly? No. Do we need to try to live in healthy relationship with the events, people and material realities of our lives? Yes."

We sisters have been living our religious vows for one year, twenty-five years, fifty years, and, yes, even seventy-five years. No matter what circumstances or changes come along, the vows give our lives their underlying stability. The practice of making vows of public commitment for the sake of religious dedication or giving oneself to God goes as far back as the Israelites and early Christianity. As time went on and religious life took on a more formal character, the church drew up canons, or rules, to govern the practice of religious poverty, chastity, and obedience. While today there is little questioning of the value of vows, there are questions about the terms used for the vows and about contemporary interpretations.

Over the past fifty years we have asked ourselves many questions related to our religious vows: How can we express the meaning of our religious vows of poverty, chastity, and obedience in ways that are consistent both with Rome's understanding and with our own experience? Should we, in fact, rename our vows to express our understanding of what we do when we commit ourselves to God as Sisters of St. Joseph? Would one vow be more appropriate than three in articulating what we do when we commit ourselves to God, to each other, and to our mission in the world? Recognizing the desire of our consociates and others to share our lives and ministries, should we consider dispensing with vows altogether and make another kind of commitment?

These questions will provoke serious discussion well into the twenty-first century. At present, we retain the three traditional vows, but we bring to them a variety of interpretations based on the ongoing reinterpretation of mission; reading of Scripture; theological insights; understanding of contemporary history, psychology, and sociology; and life experiences.

It has been said that no other group took the reforms of the Second Vatican Council as seriously as did Catholic sisters. One of the Council's documents, *Perfectae Caritatis* (1965), or "The Perfection of Charity," was addressed specifically to religious communities. We were asked to renew ourselves by identifying our founding spirit and our particular charism. Actually, our renewal started more than a decade earlier as we began to address issues surfaced by the Sister Formation Movement. It was clear that the 1917 code of canon law, which had standardized the lifestyles of religious communities, was becoming undone.

No section of our Constitution received as much vigorous discussion as the section on religious vows. The 1955 Constitution contains prescriptions for our lives that are almost entirely legal in tone. The first revision of the Constitution in 1967 reflected a remarkable change in style. Scriptural language replaced legal language. Since then we have made four revisions of our Constitution: in 1975, 1978, 1981, and 1984.

The developing changes in the church and in our personal and communal lives influenced our perception of religious vows. *Poverty* now means living a simple life, which includes the wise use of material and spiritual resources; *chastity* means developing personal relationships and living among a variety of neighbors; *obedience* means listening to the signs of the times to discern our gifts for ministry.

Our current Constitution, published in 1984, describes our religious profession as a response to the gospel. Through religious profession, we are told:

> The Spirit calls us to commit ourselves freely to the Lord and to one another in community for the sake of the kingdom. Through public vows of poverty, chastity, and obedience we promise the lifelong gift of self to the Lord for all persons without distinction. Responding in a radical way to the gospel, we direct the whole of our being to God in prayer and love, making ourselves available to share [God's] work of bringing all persons to freedom and oneness in [God]. Like Jesus, we embrace the death-life mystery that this self-emptying demands (p. 10).

It is probably our understanding of the deep meaning of the religious vow of obedience that gave us the insight and grace to renew our governance structure and our lives since the Second Vatican Council. As our current Constitution (1984) reminds us, we have embraced "both the struggle and the joy of doing what the Lord asks of us in building up the kingdom." We have indeed listened to and obeyed God's will. We have united "in community to listen to the Spirit and through prayer, dialogue, and reflection discern[ed] God's will." At the same time we have recognized "the authority of our superiors and the church" (p. 10).

By contrast a lengthy section in an earlier Constitution (1955) told us that through the religious vow of obedience we were to assume "the obligation of obeying [our] lawful superiors in all that concerns life in the institute" (p. 70). When those of us who entered the novitiate in the late 1950s and early 1960s received a copy of the Constitution, our superiors emphasized that our obedience meant obedience to them and to the Constitution. We were, in a spirit of faith, to submit our will and judgment to the will and judgment of the superior in the belief that the will of God was manifested through her. We were required to ask permission from the local superior for minor matters, from taking a walk outside the convent grounds to discarding worn clothing.

The effects of the Council and the work of the Federation research team is reflected in our 1972 interim Constitution. The approach to obedience differed in the recognition that the three vows were really one action, and this act identified our expression of "the one gift we make of ourselves to Jesus Christ in a community of love and service" (p. 4). The language now describing obedience reflected our study of Scripture and particularly of the person and mission of Jesus. It also reflected our charism, identified by the Federation research team as "profound love of God and love of neighbor without distinction."

The development of the congregation's understanding of the religious vow of obedience as reflected in the 1955, 1972, and 1984 versions of the Constitution has been quite remarkable. Rome approved the 1984 Constitution as it had approved our earlier constitutions. We see and practice obedience as carrying out Jesus' mission and as living our charism. The effects of our religious vow of obedience as we now live it are evident in the way in which we changed our whole manner of province governance and our discerning of our own ministries.

Those of us who live and work among those who are economically poor have long challenged the use of the term *poverty* in our vows. Poverty, as it is understood on the streets of our cities and towns, is not a virtue to be sought but is an evil to be overcome. Catholic teaching on social justice has, for over a century, challenged us to address the structures that perpetuate a large class of people who are economically poor. These sisters contend that professing a vow of poverty may be misleading. This point of view must be taken seriously. At the same time, the religious vow of poverty is a centuries-old tradition in the church and in religious communities. How have we understood it? Where is it leading us?

The 1955 Constitution contains fourteen entries in the "Religious Poverty" section, most of which are legal in nature. These relate to property and revenues a sister might have possessed before entering the community; the making of a will; restrictions about buying, selling, lending, or borrowing goods once vows are made; and what would happen to a sister's possessions if she left the community. At the end of this section, the spiritual meaning of poverty is articulated: the vow of poverty "relieves a religious of preoccupation in her personal needs and enables her the better to carry on special work of the congregation which is entrusted to her" (p. 78). Clearly, the focus on poverty here is on the common life. Everything was shared, and no one was more privileged than any other based on possession of goods and money. Through this common sharing, we were freed to do our work.

As we began to live in smaller groups outside of convents, we learned more about how our neighbors lived and adapted our reflections and our language about poverty. Our current Constitution (1984) reminds us that through religious poverty we respond to the "call of the Spirit by freely relinquishing the independent use and disposal of temporal goods" (p. 10). The word "independent" indicates the communal nature of our religious poverty. Christ in his self-emptying is our model. We are called to "simplicity of life which challenges us to use only what we need and to share what we have with others, especially the poor and the needy" (p. 78). This way of reflecting on poverty continues today, even as we face the dilemma of the language of poverty, given the questions about people who suffer economic poverty all around the world.

We have been able to contribute to the needs of those who are poor and to promote social justice in the world precisely because of our religious vow of poverty. Each of us has the personal responsibility to live simply and to contribute all of our efforts to the common funds of the province. In our houses and convents expenses for daily living come from our common province fund. We budget prudently and wisely for our individual, group, and province needs.

For many years the balance of income from our stipends and salaries and our expenses was precarious, to say the least. Teachers in the parochial schools relied on minimal stipends, and many other sisters "contributed services" to their ministries by taking no financial remuneration. Sister-cooks in our convents also made significant, and at times unrecognized, contributions to our convent funds through their contributed work. Because of direct payment to them, the music teachers provided us some of our funding. Sisters serving in hospitals brought in lay-equivalent salaries for many years.

As times changed, finances became a more complex matter. Through a succession of wise and prudent leaders, aided by loyal and competent business advisors, we saw the need to provide for our retirement. Meanwhile our ministries were changing as sisters had the freedom to choose new ministries to which they felt called. Changes came, of course, with the closing of parochial schools, but the greatest change came as we realized the ministry of health care had shifted into the big business of large hospitals. Unable and unwilling to compete in big business, we sold some of our hospitals. Those funds, wisely invested, have enabled us to undertake new ministries serving the "dear neighbor," to have funds to dedicate to a variety of social justice causes, and to provide for our retirement.

In the midst of an American society afflicted with materialism and consumerism, many sisters espouse the leading of a countercultural life of simplicity. Simplicity challenges us to grow in freedom from possessiveness and to share what we have with others. We sometimes see bumper stickers on province-owned cars with words like, "Live simply that others may simply live." Such words encourage us to be aware of all people who live in destitution and urge us to do what we are able to help them.

Human poverty in ourselves and others includes a variety of unfulfilled needs: cultural, intellectual, material, physical,

Members of the Earth Partners group of the province's Justice Commission work to restore the woodlands and grounds of province property.

psychological, spiritual. We are urged to eliminate whatever forms of poverty we can (Complementary Document, 1984, p. 7). Concern for the preservation of the earth's resources also belongs to the spirit of the vow of poverty. Earth Partners, a committee of sisters concerned about environmental issues, especially of our own community property, tries to make the whole community aware of our responsibility for the future of the earth.

As with the other two religious vows the vow of chastity has been vigorously discussed during the last fifty years. Every Christian is called to chastity, that is, to a life of loving and faithful relationships. What we are really promising is a vow of celibacy, a particular kind of chastity that focuses our lifestyle as unmarried women living in community. That is very different from an exclusive, long-term committed relationship.

The 1955 Constitution describes the vow of chastity as an obligation "to abstain from every interior and exterior act opposed to chastity and contrary to the sixth and ninth commandments of God." This document also exhorted us to "cultivate a spirit of self-restraint by controlling [our] thoughts and passions and by practicing mortification and self-discipline." It told us that our "conversation with seculars, especially with persons of the other sex, should be regulated by what is in accordance with business relations and social courtesy" (pp. 72–73). This suggests a spirit of caution and separation from the secular world. Within the community, we were warned to avoid "particular friendships," which were thought to be dangerous because they involved exclusive emotional attachment to another human being and might lessen the commonality of our lives.

In contrast, our current Constitution (1984) calls us to "an apostolic love which is fully human and personal" (p. 10). We are urged to develop strong community bonds and life-giving relationships. The religious vow of chastity is explicitly connected with sharing the mission of Jesus in service for others. The main focus of this vow is positive: we see ourselves as persons directing our energies toward living fully in our relationships and working for the transformation of the world.

Our focus on celibacy has shifted from the cautionary emphasis on personal chastity in the 1955 Constitution to a perception of our vow as contributing to a lifestyle of relationship and service. No matter what our sexual orientation, we live a life of celibacy. We each choose what we need to form relationships that free us to live our lives fully and revitalize us for ministry. Deep friendships have grown as we have learned to live together in a variety of settings, and these relationships are seen as healthy, humanizing, and energizing gifts in our lives.

In the years since the Second Vatican Council we have reflected deeply on the meaning of our vows. Our discussions have been passionate, exciting, and sometimes painful. The questions remain: Will the vows, as we name them today, endure through the twenty-first century? Do the words *poverty, chastity,* and *obedience* adequately describe the commitment we make when we join our lives with the Sisters of St. Joseph?

The Constitution reminds us in the conclusion to the section on religious vows that "the Spirit calls us to live out our consecration in community, and with the strength that comes from our life together, to turn beyond ourselves to serve a world in need. We love freely. We live simply. We listen attentively. Thus we realize our commitment to Jesus Christ, . . . giving ourselves to others" (p. 11).

This call of the Spirit, of course, is always a challenge. We are called to be countercultural: to live our religious vow of poverty in a culture often characterized by consumerism and economic injustice; to live our religious vow of chastity in a culture where sex is often exploited; to live our religious vow of obedience in a culture in which power is often used to dominate rather than empower others. The vows do not ask us to live *out* of the world but to live our mission *in* the world.

8

Seeking God

LINES FROM THE POEM "The Veil and the Rock," by Sister Alice Gustava (Maris Stella) Smith, well-known poet and former teacher of creative writing at the College of St. Catherine, show her profound insight into the sacramental nature of the earth and the variety of ways in which God is present in our lives. These lines serve as a signpost on the inner journey many Sisters of St. Joseph have taken over the past fifty years:

> I have found, in many syllables the Word speaks. Of what I
>   heard
> at first I had understood only this much:
> Come follow. All else is hollow.
> The why, the wherefore, none of this I knew,
> but in the woods the blue gentians
> blown from stems the color of wine
> shine more terribly, now, than armies in array (p. 89).

Although the poem tells of Sister Alice's own spiritual journey, like most personal stories it awakens us to our own experiences and becomes universal. These lines offer a way to reflect on the movement from responding to God's call to recognizing God's presence in the world. Sister Alice's words introduce the notions of finding, of understanding, of growing and changing within the revelatory image of gentians in the spring woods.

Earlier in her poem Sister Alice writes, "But now I know with my mind and not my instinct." If these early ways of seeing God continue in our lives, it is partly because they are the instinctive ways of a child. But knowing "with my mind" means understanding what Sister Alice calls "the why, the wherefore." Our experiences as Catholic women and as Sisters of St. Joseph have been that holiness is found in ordinary daily living.

Thinking about God is a reflective process, a matter of recognizing underlying images and assumptions and finding language and symbols to uncover and speak them. Speaking *about* God is not the same as praying or talking *to* God, however closely they may be related.

Sister Alice Gustava Smith stands near the south side of Our Lady of Victory Chapel at the College of St. Catherine. She was a beloved teacher of creative writing and literature to many generations of students.

The images that arise from within us or are recognized as symbols outside ourselves are roots and sources for Christian faith and give rise both to reflecting about God (theology) and talking to God (spirituality). Many of the images that continue to inform our theology and spirituality took root in childhood and were shaped by our families and backgrounds.

In reflecting on her religious background Sister Vera Chester, who was a convert to Catholicism during her college years, said recently: "My religious connections were formed more by carpools than convictions or commitments. My parents were not church-going people, but they, together with the parents of most of my friends in suburban Chicago, took turns seeing that their children went to some sort of Protestant Sunday school. I was christened by a Norwegian Lutheran pastor when I was a few weeks old, went to Methodist Sunday school when I visited my grandma in Ohio (she didn't go, she just sent me with the neighbor kids), and then joined the choir first in an Episcopalian and then a Presbyterian congregation."

Sister Vera goes on to say, "My childhood religious associations have mostly to do with prayers before bedtime, images from the Bible (especially the Psalms and Old Testament stories), and music (from "Jesus Loves Me" to four-part hymns, from Palestrina polyphony to Bach oratorios). Perhaps because of my flexible church relationships, which in my teen years stretched to include visits to Jewish synagogues with my best friend and occasional Catholic masses with my stepmother and brothers, I have always accepted that there are many ways of imaging and approaching God." In her ministry as a college professor of theology, Sister Vera has spent her life teaching students to value those "many ways."

For those of us who were "cradle Catholics" our early experiences of religion were quite different. Born into a French Catholic family in rural North Dakota, Sister Grace Saumur was surrounded from her infancy by Catholicism. Among her earliest memories as a child was how cold her toes felt on the ten-mile ride to church for Mass every Sunday. For French Catholics Sunday was a very special day. Sister Grace wore Sunday clothes and enjoyed a big dinner with her family.

Sunday meant no work in the fields for adults and lots of play and fun for everyone in her close-knit Catholic community.

In preparation for her first Holy Communion Sister Grace received a book with a picture of Jesus on the cross. When she asked her mother, "Did Jesus really die for me?" and her mother said, "Yes," she was so impressed with such generosity that she dates the beginning of her vocation to religious life to that time. The realization of God's generosity and love for her have formed the mainstay of her prayer and spirituality in her ministries of elementary school teacher, certified music specialist, province secretary, and originator and organizer of the prayer partner ministry at the College of St. Catherine.

Like Sisters Vera and Grace, whatever our ministry, we each bring to the community a unique story of our early experiences of God. What we hold in common is our desire to journey together toward a closer union with God.

The early spiritual foundation we received during our novitiate years in the community has proved solid and lasting. Our study of Scripture nourished in us a love of the many and diverse scriptural images of God such as shepherd, king, potter, wisdom, mother, as well as wind and word. We deepened our understanding of the stories in the Hebrew and Christian Scriptures of God's action in history and of Jesus Christ as the center of Christian faith. As a community we express our communal faith in rituals and words that spring from our interactions with each other and with those among whom we serve. For our first sisters in Le Puy and for us today, community, ministry, and prayer come together as one. Our current Constitution (1984) describes our prayer as "a living relationship with God—a relationship moving and growing with the rhythms of life. In prayer we open ourselves to the transforming power of the risen Lord who calls us to share his life and friendship and to seek the love, the will and the glory of God" (p. 12).

We have developed new prayer rituals in recent years for province gatherings that are rooted in our communal memory and reflect new expressions of our relationship with God. Prayer is integral in each of our gatherings, whether congregational chapter, Province Assembly, or committee meeting. In our community prayer we often sing music ranging from Gregorian chant to contemporary songs, some of them composed by our sisters. Dance, movement, and colorful banners sometimes add vitality to our celebrations.

Our sense of the sacred has led us to new insights and a deeper sense of sacramentality. We value a sacramental vision of life, recognizing that all is holy—seasons of the year, seasons of life, seasons of death and resurrection. Every moment is a sacramental moment. As we sometimes sing at community gatherings: "Every part of this earth is to my people holy."

Some of the changes in forms of community prayer in recent decades brought pain for some sisters who preferred more traditional prayer. Other sisters spoke of experiencing a new authenticity in their prayer lives. Daily Eucharist remains central to the lives of many of us. However, the Eucharist, proclaimed by the Second Vatican Council as both sign and source of Christian unity, has caused division among us, as it has among other Catholics, because women are not considered to be officially equal in eucharistic ministry. Church theology teaches the equality of all the baptized, but church discipline and practice continue to deny the full equality of women.

Christian Scriptures make it clear that the Holy Spirit can give gifts to whomever the Spirit chooses. These gifts are not to be buried, either by the person or by the community—or by a church that sometimes does not value gifts given to women. Our sisters function as leaders of community prayer and as guides in spiritual direction. The leadership we have assumed in community and ministry has made it possible for us to be actively engaged in church renewal. Our community's insistence that preparation for religious life should include theological and liturgical education helped us to take on new liturgical and ecclesiastical roles with confidence. We are called upon to give scriptural reflections at the Sunday eucharistic liturgy at Bethany Convent, at funerals for our sisters and parishioners, and at community celebrations.

Our sisters and consociates have planned our rituals for entrance into the community and for funeral liturgies. Each occasion can reflect the story of the individual and the story of the community. For example, Sister Mary Judith Stoughton, who died in 1991, gave this description of the funeral she hoped to have: "Make it all an experience of 'kindom.' Be sure the texts are all in inclusive language and all point to the glory and praise of God. Funerals are for the church to grow. I want it to be an experience of reconciliation. Have fun and make it beautiful."

A life-filled ritual marked the last change of province leadership in the twentieth century as we looked back by giving thanks for the outgoing leadership team and council and looked forward by offering support to new leadership. The music, readings, and symbolic gestures and gifts reflected our connectedness with God's creation, with the change of seasons, and with one another. The liminal moment between the past and the future was honored with silence. Sister Maureen Freeman, liaison of the congregational leadership team to the St. Paul Province, commissioned the new team and council by reminding all of us assembled that "our mission is that of the church: to continue the mission of Jesus." Echoing our Constitution, she expanded on what our mission means: to heal and reconcile, to serve all persons without distinction, to make known through our lives the gospel we proclaim, to enable others to assume an active responsibility for building the reign of God, to recognize and defend the human dignity of all persons, and to promote justice with a particular concern for those living in poverty.

The vitality of this commissioning of our 1999–2004 leadership team was not unlike that of our first three-day summer gathering in 1982, a time for prayer, reflection, renewal, and recreation. We called this 1982 gathering "A Little Design for the Future." Since then we have had two similar gatherings, in 1988 and 1992, and plan another three-day gathering in August 2001 to celebrate our 150th anniversary in St. Paul.

At the 1982 gathering we came together after two decades of tension during which we had changed our clothing, our names, and indeed our vision of religious life. In the process we had often found ourselves polarized and in need of reconciliation. A ritual of reconciliation did much to heal us as a community.

During this ritual we asked forgiveness of each other. Those of us who had held positions of authority stood to ask forgiveness "for exercising my authority in a way that made you feel powerless . . . for hiding behind the rules rather than being sensitive to human needs . . . for not allowing

Mary Kaye Medinger, consociate and director of Wisdom Ways, dances at a celebration of the liturgy during the August Days of 1992.

you to participate in decisions that affected your life." After an emotional pause the rest of us responded: "I welcome this opportunity to tell you—I forgive you—and may grace, mercy, and peace be yours through Christ our God." Then we went on to acknowledge areas for which each of us in turn stood in need of forgiveness. In a period of silence, together we washed our hands in bowls of water brought from various bodies of water representing our historical journey. When this action of reconciliation was complete, we prayed together: "We thank you, God, for being a God of mercy and compassion and for giving us the power to forgive one another. We ask that the reconciliation we celebrate this evening continues to permeate our lives. We ask this in the name of Jesus the Lord."

Through our rituals we pray for justice in the world and try to express a globally inclusive awareness that is "for you and for all." Our community extends the hospitality of Christ to family, friends, and neighbors who gather with us on occasions like Sunday vespers during Advent.

In our annual retreats we seek to meet God in solitude and prayer. Instead of sitting in hard pews as we did in the past at the traditional preached retreats in the chapel at the College of St. Catherine, some of us have found new ways of encountering God. We go to nearby retreat centers for preached, directed, or private retreats. We can find God within ourselves and in creation—at the ocean and at lakesides, in the mountain or woods. We resonate with Henry Thoreau when he says in *Walden Pond*, "I went to the woods because I wished to live deliberately."

Some of us go alone or in small groups to Timberlee, our province's rustic lodge on Big Fish Lake, the Dwelling in the Woods, a retreat center in northern Minnesota founded by our sisters, or our small cabin at White Ash Lake in Wisconsin. In the years when the Sisters of St. Joseph operated a House of

Prayer in Stillwater, Minnesota, many of us treasured its beautiful and prayerful space, not only for retreats but also for occasional days of the quiet hospitality provided by the small group
of sisters who formed a core community there.

Our lives and our struggles witness to the depth and outcome of our renewal processes in prayer and spirituality. As a
province community and as individual members, we have
embraced the work of renewal with the independent, creative,
and populist energy we inherited from our pioneer sisters. We
have joined with our lay sisters and brothers in parish renewal programs and spirituality movements. Centering prayer, an
age-old method leading to contemplative prayer that is experiencing a new popularity, has attracted some of us. Praying the
rosary, reflecting on Scripture, and reciting contemporary
forms of the Liturgy of the Hours or Divine Office continue to
be foundational in the prayer lives of many of us.

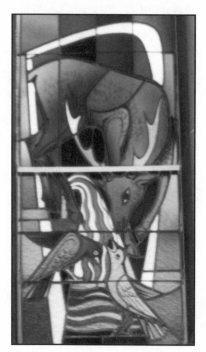

At recent congregational and
provincial chapter gatherings we
have reaffirmed our commitment
to the meaning of justice in all of
life. Our spirituality involves all
aspects of justice, which calls us
to be in right relationship with
God, with creation, with the peoples of the earth, and with one
another. We aim to deepen our
understanding of global systems of
domination, to transform these

*Among the stained glass windows in the
Bethany Chapel the lower portion of this
window represents contemplative prayer
through the symbols of a deer seeking living water and birds singing praise to God.*

systems, and to promote the fullness of life. We continue to be mindful that our spirituality cannot be separated from our identity as Sisters of St. Joseph and the gospel call to be one with our neighbors.

In our personal journeys and the journey of our religious community, we walk with the whole church and all peoples of the earth. For us as sisters and consociates the journey is one of rediscovering roots, understanding the signs of the times, and recommitting ourselves together to an uncertain future. Even as we have been searching for the meaning of our being together, each of us has undertaken the journey as an individual pilgrimage. It is a spiritual pilgrimage flowing from commitment and undertaken in fidelity and hope, evidenced not only by our ministries but also by our prayer.

In our seeking for God and for understanding of who we are, where we are going, and what is asked of us, the Word sings within us, as Sister Alice reminds us at the end of her poem:

> There is left then only the Word
> in the heart's hush heard,
> a bird singing under the dark
> that will never stop singing (p. 90).

9

Ministering as Artists

W HEN WE CREATE, WE ARE ONE with each other, and one with ourselves." These words of Sister Ansgar Holmberg, one of our visual artists, remind us that art is a spiritual experience. When we create or enjoy the arts we are touched by beauty and joy. Both the visual arts and music help us to be more human, more sensitive, and closer to the infinite. They contribute to the development of our social consciousness and do their part to bring harmony into our world.

Sister Joanne Emmer, another of our visual artists, believes that artists make the invisible visible so that others may be led to mystery. In this sense art is a form of spirituality that has touched all of us but most particularly the sisters who have ministered in the arts by teaching, creating, and performing.

Our art and music teachers have been involved in these ministries since our beginnings in Minnesota. St. Agatha's Conservatory of Music and Art, founded in 1884, earned the reputation of being the finest institution of its kind in the Midwest. There, for seventy-eight years, succeeding generations of Sisters of St. Joseph provided instruction in such arts as china painting and dramatic arts as well as piano and violin. The conservatory was home not only for artists and musicians but also for sisters teaching in nearby grade schools. The conservatory had been founded to house these sisters and to provide much-needed income, which St. Agatha's shared with the province at large.

As Sister Ann Thomasine Sampson points out in *The History of St. Agatha's Conservatory of Music and Art*, that institution—founded, administered, and staffed by a group of women long before the presence of a woman's movement—was unique in the history of women's religious congregations throughout the United States and Canada.

Sister St. Margaret Jordan, who had been teaching music for fifty-eight years, half of them at St. Agatha's when it closed in 1962, saw to the meticulous details of a sale, which included the disposition of the conservatory's collection of copies of famous paintings made by sisters who had traveled to Europe to study art. This was in the days before easy reproduction of great paintings.

Promoting the arts was also one of the earliest traditions at the College of St. Catherine. The first president of the college, Sister Antonia McHugh, vigorously promoted art and music as essential components of education. The long-time chair of the art department, Sister Philomene McAuley, incorporated the aims of the Catholic Art Association to revive Christian art, especially in our churches, and to improve the teaching of art in our Catholic schools and college.

The visual arts thrived not only at the conservatory and the college but also in the high schools and in the novitiate. In the novitiate of the 1950s our art was different from the portrait, landscape, and china painting traditions of St. Agatha's. Works were identified by date and place of composition and generally not by name. The arts were not considered so much a ministry as a part of our life and work.

The chief proponent of a new sacred art for group after group of aspiring sisters was Sister Cyril Clare Casey. As a liturgy instructor, she urged the novices to create works reflecting the simplicity of line, strong colors, and mild distortions of earlier Christian times and to spurn the nineteenth-century styles of the immigrant churches most of us had all grown up in. She taught us that beauty and truth are one and that sound theology is expressed through sound art. To ensure that we understood this concept, she required that all novice-designed projects be submitted to her for approval.

"Everyone is a special kind of artist," Sister Cyril Clare wrote in an issue of *Catholic Art Quarterly*. This was true whether the medium was calligraphy, leather tooling, posters, pageantry, drama, cards, or the only arts required of every sister in the novitiate, elocution, singing, and sewing. The arts permeated our lives and enabled us to celebrate the liturgical year more fully. Sister Cyril Clare's influence was deep, and to this day, upon the completion of some creative endeavor, one of us can be heard to say, "Wouldn't Cyril Clare be proud!"

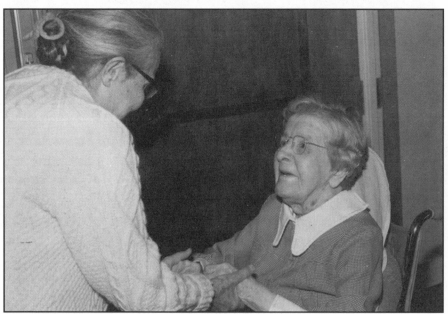

Sister Cyril Clare Casey in her later years with her long-time friend, artist Ade Bethune.

Novices of the 1950s and 1960s were immersed in the liturgical movement, which opened their eyes to waves of social change like pacifism, feminism, and civil rights. The ferment of *The Catholic Worker* newspaper and the art of Ade Bethune, a dynamic liturgical artist, permeated novitiate studies.

The attic of the novitiate was a refuge for art makers. An article in *Beginnings* (January 8, 1969, p. 95), a community newsletter, tells of the "coffeehouse creativity" that took place there: "The affiliates, novices and young professed sisters gathered in the attic to ponder Scripture passages and try to interpret them creatively in writing, drama, audio-visual, music and art workshops." We were becoming more aware that "before art can be Christian, it must first be human." Some of the artists who left the community continue to create expressing the principles they learned in the novitiate.

Classroom teachers enjoyed courses in basic design taught at the College of St. Catherine on Saturdays. They brought what they learned there into their classrooms. These teachers used a program developed by Sister Marie Pierre Benoit, a province art supervisor, which included art appreciation studies. Children in grades one through eight received small reproductions of classic art. By the end of eighth grade, each child had studied forty masterpieces. Music appreciation and art were frequently combined, and children's creations brightened the classrooms.

Today more sisters than ever, from novices to retired sisters, are involved in art of all kinds. Quietly integrated into everyday living, their art has its impact on others as it finds its way into the small gift shops at Carondelet Center, the former novitiate building, or at Bethany Convent. Sister Mary Lou Murray's original quilting is having a special impact. With sixteen women at St. Peter Claver Church in St. Paul, she created a quilt that is now at the reconstructed slave ship, the *Amistad*, in Mystic Seaport, Connecticut.

The August Days of the 1980s, the Celebration Through the Arts series of the 1990s, and our festivals and fairs have featured concerts and poetry readings, dance and drama, and exhibits by card designers, candle carvers, photographers, posters, quilters, and bakers. Our art making is a way of being present to others and is never more powerful than when we combine our many expressions into community rituals.

Many of us owe our recognition of the value of the arts in our lives to our connection with the College of St. Catherine. Well before the ecumenical movement, Sister Mary Judith Stoughton's influence extended beyond the college. She explored and taught the relationship between art and the spirituality of other cultures, especially early Christian, East Asian, and American Indian. She served as art editor of the *New Catholic Encyclopedia* and did editorial work for *Catholic Art Quarterly*. Her friendship with Ade Bethune resulted in the establishment of the Ade Bethune collection in the library at St. Catherine's and in Sister Judith's biography, *Proud Donkey of Schaerbeek, Ade Bethune, Catholic Worker Artist,* published in 1988.

The Mother Antonia McHugh Fine Arts Complex on the college campus has served to celebrate all the arts since its opening in the 1970s. The art building houses the Catherine G. Murphy Gallery, which displays a wide variety of artwork, especially by women, including some of the work of Sisters of St. Joseph. From time to time the foyer of the library also displays works of sister-artists, both past and present.

Recent exhibits of the paintings of two retired professors at St. Catherine's demonstrate their continuing creativity. The connection between painting and poetry come together in the work of Sister Magdalen (Marie David) Schimanski from the art department and Sister Mary Virginia Micka from the English department. Both artists have published poems in journals and chapbooks. Sister Mary Virginia served as poetry editor of

Sisters Today, a magazine for women religious. She has developed a small industry of her watercolor cards and paintings, and Sister Joanne Emmer has interpreted her poems through colorful silk-screen designs.

Sister Magdalen provided the woodcut illustrations to accompany a volume of Christmas poems by another sister-poet, Sister Alice Gustava (Maris Stella) Smith. This volume and *Body of Time*, a collection of Sister Ellen Murphy's poems, were among the beautifully designed Christmas books of North Central Publishing in St. Paul.

Considered by many to be our poet laureate, Sister Alice published many poems over the years. Those from her two earlier volumes, *Here Only a Dove* and *Frost for Saint Brigid*, were gathered into *Collected Poems* in 1992 by the St. Catherine's Alumnae Association as a tribute to her many years as professor of English and beloved teacher of creative writing. Her poems show her deep sense of the sacred in the simplest things of life. "It Is the Reed," the initial sonnet in the collection, reveals her own view of poets as instruments of divine inspiration:

> From out the peaceful hollow of its throat
> such music pours as I am unaware
> how to devise. I did not think these things.
> It is the reed that sings.

Two siblings, Sisters Kathleen and Ansgar Holmberg, have integrated their lives as artists with their earlier ministries of elementary teaching and pastoral/spirituality ministries. Sister Kathleen's specialty is the ancient art of the religious icon. Through workshops with experts in the United States and Russia, along with continuous independent study, she is perfecting her skill in creating luminous religious images. Among them is an icon of St. Catherine of Alexandria,

Under the watchful eye of St. Catherine of Alexandria, Sister Kathleen Holmberg creates a new icon.

patron saint of the College of St. Catherine. Sister Ansgar, illustrator for *Eyes Open on a World*, produces many paintings, designs, and illustrations. Her rich and colorful paintings evoke consciousness of our bond with all peoples and with the earth and our responsibility to use its gifts wisely.

The pottery of Sister Jean Nelson is treasured and used at many a eucharistic and family meal. Many of her elegant pieces are created to serve purely as objects of contemplation. She has passed on her skill as a potter to many students not only at St. Catherine's but also for more than twenty years at Potters' House on the ground floor of Carondelet Center. This busy place serves both as school and studio.

After spending most of her professional career teaching at the College of St. Catherine, Sister Joanne Emmer continues as a prolific painter and printmaker. A unique contribution to her teaching of art is the course she designed as a way for students

A ceramic pot takes form under Sister Jean Nelson's hands.

who are blind to fulfill their course requirement in the fine arts. All participants, whether sighted or visually impaired, wear blindfolds for every session and learn through touch to create and release the imagination.

Music is also an art that develops discipline, concentration, and imagination. It is Plato who said, "Music gives a soul to the universe, wings to the mind, flight to the imagination, a charm to sadness, gaiety and life to everything." Our musicians share their music so that others may experience the beauty and joy of an ineffable art.

A young woman entering the novitiate in the 1950s found music for worship dominated by Gregorian chant. Pope Pius X's encyclical, *Motu Proprio* (1903), called for congregational singing at Mass and for the revival of chant. But sacred music did not hold a monopoly in the novitiate. Recreation hours were often enlivened by community singing and square dancing. The novices created

Sister Joanne Emmer (right)
watches her students sculpt
their own heads. Even the
sighted students are "blind" in
this class.

original and often hilarious skits with music and at times those proficient in classical music performed on their instruments.

The choir director and teacher of courses in Gregorian chant in the novitiate, Sister Helen Dolores Sweeney, also taught elementary school music there as well as at the St. Paul Diocesan Teachers College and at the College of St. Catherine. Highly respected in her field, she gave many talks for school associations and other groups throughout Minnesota. Her book of poems, *Older Than Trees,* reflects her deep spirituality. From 1940 to 1962, Sister Helen Dolores had the challenging job of music supervisor for some fifty elementary schools in the St. Paul Province.

In a parallel position, Sister Carlos Eue served as supervisor of precollege piano teachers from the 1950s until 1972. When she began supervising, seventy-five sisters gave piano lessons, but the number declined during subsequent years. Earlier Sister Carlos had chaired the large music department at St. Joseph's Academy in St. Paul, which offered for academic credit lessons in piano and voice, supplemented by theory courses. Each year almost a hundred students studied and practiced regularly at the school. St. Joseph's became known

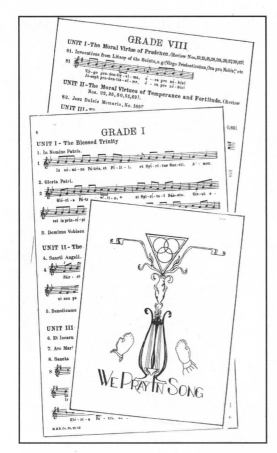

Sister Helen Dolores Sweeney organized a course of study on Gregorian chant for elementary school students. While the chants were taught in Latin, each teacher was responsible for providing an English translation. Sister Helen Dolores developed the curriculum so that students could more fully participate in the liturgies of the church year.

for outstanding two-piano recitals and for concerts at which students played concertos with members of the Minneapolis (later Minnesota) Symphony Orchestra.

The St. Joseph's Academy Glee Club, founded by Sister Ann Thomasine Sampson in 1937, won acclaim for its performances. Sister Ann Thomasine coped well with the policy that sisters did not perform in public. She accomplished the feat of directing the annual performance of the *Messiah* from a piano on stage with the keyboard and herself hidden from the audience by the curtains.

Our other high schools also thrived as centers for music. The flourishing music department of St. John's Academy in Jamestown, North Dakota, which brought in visiting artists, served as a cultural center for the surrounding area. The Academy of the Holy Angels in Minneapolis had both a fine music department and a very successful program in theater and speech under the direction of Sister Charitas Farr. To this day its success in preparing students in theater continues the work she began.

Beginning in the 1950s the province sent a number of sisters to earn master's degrees or to take summer courses in music at such institutions as the Eastman School of Music and Pius X School of Liturgical Music, both in New York.

In the 1960s all of us experienced the effects of the revolution in liturgical music encouraged by the Second Vatican Council. The Council's *Constitution on the Sacred Liturgy* admitted use of good music from a variety of cultures and allowed use of the vernacular in the liturgy. After the Council, when good contemporary church music was scarce, several of our musicians contributed to the new repertory of music for worship. Sister Mary Davida Wood published one of the first Masses in English after the Second Vatican Council, *Mass in Honor of Mary, Tower of David*, which was performed throughout the United States and in Japan. Sister Catherine (Lucina) Kessler, an expert in Gregorian chant, provided English texts for celebrations throughout the liturgical year. For years these sisters, both College of St. Catherine faculty members, as a piano/organ and violin duo, delighted audiences with their performances of other types of music.

As a faculty member at St. Catherine's, Sister Mary Ann (Nathaniel) Hanley addressed a justice issue in her work with piano pedagogy. Her aim was to offset the lack of state education requirements for piano teachers, which resulted in many unqualified teachers. To promote professionalism, in 1962 she instituted St. Catherine's piano pedagogy program, one of the first in the country, which later became a certificate program. As president of the Minnesota Music Teachers Association (MMTA) she also initiated the upgrading of MMTA certification

Sister Mary Davida Wood at the piano and Sister Catherine Kessler with her violin were performers and accompanists for many groups.

requirements. Sister Mary Ann extended her ministry overseas, doing research in West Africa and making presentations at piano teachers' conferences in Europe.

After two years studying with Shinichi Suzuke in Japan and becoming a certified Suzuki specialist, Sister Patricia Binko founded the Carondelet Suzuki Talent Education School for Strings in St. Paul in 1986. Earlier she had founded and directed the Church Women's United Ecumenical Choir and played violin in the Grand Forks Symphony Orchestra.

The St. Joseph School of Music in St. Paul was founded by Sisters Georgine Nugent and Rosemary Hayes in 1971, the year that St. Joseph's Academy closed. The sisters aimed to continue the tradition of excellence of the academy's music department. The St. Joseph School of Music has expanded under the leadership of Sister Rose Immacula Brennan, its director since 1982, and has moved from its home in the former novitiate building to more spacious quarters. The enrollment has grown to over 1,200 students of all ages and levels and the faculty to forty-eight teachers, including thirteen with doctorates. The school offers instruction in many instruments, voice, theory, and composition and provides classes for young children.

Today, although there are far fewer music teachers than in the years when almost every convent had at least one, our sisters serve as song leaders and choir members in parishes. The legacy of our music teachers lives on in their many students, who teach, perform, direct choirs, compose music, or simply enjoy it. Joy is the gift that our artists and musicians have brought to their students and to all of us.

"Sleeves Rolled Up"

10

Teaching the Mind and Heart

T HOSE FIRST FOUR SISTERS OF ST. JOSEPH who taught in a log cabin on the banks of the Mississippi River could never have dreamed how their successors would expand their small beginnings. Like our pioneer sisters we have embraced our ministry of teaching with energy and determination. From the beginning we have reached out to where we were needed, coped with changing situations, and let go of cherished institutions when circumstances required it. We now work with new groups of people desiring an education.

By the time of our centenary celebration in 1951, 428 of our sisters taught 17,224 elementary students in forty-nine parochial schools. On the secondary level, 114 sisters instructed 2,430 students in ten high schools or academies. Fifty years later, in 2001, only nine sisters were involved in education: seven at the elementary level and two at the secondary level. Many forces, both external and internal, brought about this change.

In many ways the 1950s and early 1960s were golden years for Catholic education. We participated in educational conferences held nationally by the Congregation of the Sisters of St. Joseph of Carondelet. We asked: Are our teachers sufficiently prepared to teach the social doctrine of the church at any level—elementary, secondary, college. We discussed the radical changes in curricula on all levels caused by the explosion of knowledge.

Yet, our elementary and secondary schools operated much like those of earlier decades. Stability and predictability punctuated each day's routine. Because experienced teachers mentored younger teachers, common expectations and values were passed on to succeeding generations. For many years province educational supervisors visited schools to evaluate curricula and instructional methods of experienced and beginning teachers.

Sisters Mary Ellen Cameron and De Lourdes McAulay were two such supervisors. Working with Monsignor Roger Connole, a visionary educator and superintendent of schools for the archdiocese, they developed an educational model that integrated curriculum units in religion and social studies. Through this model, Sisters Mary Ellen and De Lourdes changed the parochial educational system not only for the Archdiocese of St. Paul and Minneapolis but also for the dioceses of New Ulm in southern Minnesota and Fargo in North Dakota.

Later Sisters Aline Baumgartner and Jean Ann Eckes, along with Monsignor Connole, developed *The Christian Inheri-*

tance series (Liturgical Press, 1963), a program of religious education for elementary school students that came to be used nationwide. For years teachers taught the program from mimeographed copies. In the 1960s it was

A rendering of Sister Mary Ellen Cameron by Sister Francis Joseph (Susan) Shukay, a former member of the province.

published in book format and included full-color illustrations done by two of our artists, Sisters Ansgar Holmberg and Joanne Emmer. *The Christian Inheritance* series provided a valuable resource to students for integrating religion into their lives.

Our sisters were aware of accelerating church and societal changes in the 1950s and 1960s and their corresponding impact on educational efforts. Many were admired and respected for their leadership during this time. Sister Carolyn Wittmann was one such educator. Like other sisters she was committed to the social teaching of the church. This was most obvious in the respect she gave, and expected others to give, to each human being of different cultural backgrounds and economic classes. In the 1950s, while principal at Nativity Grade School in St. Paul—and years before the changes of the Second Vatican Council—she arranged for parts of the Mass to be celebrated in English to help students understand its importance in their lives.

By the mid-1960s the Catholic population was growing in numbers and affluence. Graduates of an earlier Catholic school system had become professionals in various fields. They moved to the suburbs, where a few parishes built new schools and many set up comprehensive religious education programs in place of schools. The last two schools we agreed to staff were Good Shepherd Middle School and St. Joseph's Elementary School, both in suburban areas of the Twin Cities.

The influx of societal changes also affected the sisters teaching in rural Minnesota. Farming communities began to see a dramatic decrease in family farms when parents with young children moved to larger cities, where they could take advantage of more opportunities. Some rural schools closed. St. Mary's Academy in Graceville, Minnesota, which had opened in 1885 as a boarding and day school for children of Irish immigrants and American Indians, closed its high school in 1959 and its grade school ten years later. Limited financial resources and the availability of teachers in a small rural area made the closings necessary.

In some parishes different religious communities of women were responsible at different times for the same parish school. The staff at John Ireland School (formerly St. Peter's) in St. Peter, Minnesota, consisted at times of the Sisters of St. Francis; the Sisters of St. Joseph of Carondelet, St. Paul Province; or the School Sisters of Notre Dame, Mankato Province. (See Raiche and Biermaier for the story of sisters who taught in parochial schools in Minnesota.) When Sister Clare Bloms became principal in 1982, she brought three other Sisters of St. Joseph to teach in the school. A creative educational leader, Sister Clare wanted both to make learning a joy and to ensure that the school had the support of the civic community. She believed in individually guided education and found ways to bring out the best personal qualities in each teacher and student. Other parochial and public administrators in the area admired the schools she administered and often asked her to provide in-service programs for their staffs.

Some of our sisters returned to rural Minnesota during their active retirement years. After Sister Gregory Sanger retired from teaching at St. Edward's School in Minneota, she continued to work at the school for another fourteen years as a remedial reading and math teacher; she also staffed the school library. In her book *All God's Children Have Brains*, Sister Gregory quoted Charles Dickens, whose philosophy reflected her own: "I love these little people, and it is not a slight thing when they, who are so fresh from God, love us" (p. ix).

As plans developed for school consolidations both in rural Minnesota and in the Twin Cities during the 1960s and 1970s, experienced teachers and administrators took leadership roles. Project Discovery, a consolidation of six Catholic schools near downtown St. Paul, was the dream of three of these schools' principals, all Sisters of St. Joseph: Sisters Monica (Mary Helen) Frederick, Frances Mary Benz, and Catherine Hare. The sisters, dissatisfied with the methods and curricula of the traditional school, wrote a proposal in 1968 that suggested consolidation and a new educational model focused on individualized and sensory learning experiences to meet the needs of the children. Part of the excitement of Project Discovery was the racially and culturally mixed school population. Children from French, German, Irish, and Polish backgrounds studied and played with Mexican, African American, Native American, and Asian children.

Because of personnel shortages in religious communities and insufficient financial resources for parishes, the archdiocese announced in January 1971 that a number of Catholic elementary schools in Minneapolis and St. Paul would close at the end of the school year and that other schools would be consolidated. Highland Catholic School, a consolidation of three elementary schools in St. Paul formerly staffed by our sisters, remains one of the most long-lived and successful school consolidations. In South Minneapolis, Christ the King–St. Thomas is an example of a school consolidation that has faced special challenges but that exists today as a successful venture.

Commenting on the radical changes in elementary education since 1951, Sister Victoria Houle said, "Changes in Catholic schools reflected changes in society and in the church. Instruction moved from adherence to diocesan units and approved textbooks to a broader choice of materials to meet student needs. The computer launched an information explosion, which has revolutionized teaching and research at all levels of education. Catholic social teachings and Christian beliefs must be continually integrated into the fabric of instruction and life of the learning community." Sister Victoria was directly involved in these changes as a teacher, administrator, chair of the education department at the College of St. Catherine, and finally supervisor of elementary education for the Archdiocese of St. Paul and Minneapolis.

The role of our province in secondary education has been similar to our involvement in elementary education. In the 1950s and early 1960s our sisters taught in six parish-owned high schools: St. Anthony's in Minneapolis, St. Mary's Academy in Graceville, St. Mary's in Waverly, St. Mary's in Bird Island, and Holy Redeemer (Central Catholic) in Marshall, all in Minnesota, and at St. John's Academy in Jamestown, North Dakota. In the Twin Cities we owned and staffed four high schools: St. Joseph's Academy and Derham Hall High School in St. Paul and St. Margaret's Academy and the Academy of the Holy Angels in Minneapolis. We also owned and staffed the Academy of St. James in Grand Forks until 1960, when ownership of the school was transferred to area parishes.

Changes affected secondary schools as they had elementary schools. Sister Julie Boo, supervisor of secondary education in our schools, recalls the late 1960s and early 1970s as a time of rising educational costs, declining enrollments, and increasing competition from public schools. If our schools were to survive, teachers and administrators needed to develop innovative programs. In addition, most of our schools were for girls, and some parents questioned the value of single-sex education.

Province-owned schools gave us more independence and responsibility in coping with change. Plans for a new St. Margaret's Academy to replace the original building, an old brownstone mansion near downtown Minneapolis, went back as far as the mid-1940s. The new school opened on a twenty-eight-acre site on the western edge of Minneapolis in 1960. Sister Patricia Heslin, an English teacher at both the old and new schools, often told students about St. Margaret, Queen of Scotland. "She had a lot of influence on that headstrong husband-king of hers," said Sister Patricia, the implication being that the students, too, could be leaders. In the early 1970s, the Sisters of St. Joseph and the Christian Brothers began to discuss the merger of St. Margaret's and Benilde, a neighboring boys' school, because of low student enrollments at both schools.

Later, another high school merger occurred in St. Paul between Derham Hall High School, a college preparatory school for girls, and Cretin High School, a comprehensive school with a military program for boys. Planning for the merger began in 1985 and was completed in 1987. The boards and staffs drew up vision, philosophy, and goal statements and curricula were combined. Three years later, according to Sister Susan Oeffling, then co-principal, the Sisters of St. Joseph questioned whether the community should continue to sponsor the school,

Sister Judith Kavanaugh is one of two sisters involved in secondary education today. A teacher of Spanish and Latin at Cretin-Derham Hall, she also served as principal of Derham Hall High School for three years.

in part because of attitudes toward women. Discussion among sister–staff members and the Province Council resulted in the decision to maintain our commitment and to work toward gender equality. Cretin-Derham Hall today is thriving and is the school of choice for many young people.

Both St. Margaret's and Derham Hall High School became coeducational when they merged with boys' schools and moved to new locations. The Academy of the Holy Angels, faced with the possibility of closing, became coed on its current site in 1972. Three years earlier Sister Katherine Egan and Reverend Robert Cassidy, co-principals, had initiated a new concept in school administration—that of team leadership. The fund-raising campaign that they launched helped meet rising

Sister Bernadine Reinhard spent fifty-eight years in teaching, thirty-five of them at the Academy of the Holy Angels. "By observing the world around us, we learn so much," she often told her students. "By using our imagination we can create, and through our creations we can see the reflection of God." (M. Picot and Associates, Forest Hills, New York)

school expenses and increased the school's visibility in South Minneapolis, where it continues to be a sought-after secondary education option. Our sisters continue to be represented on the school boards of the Academy of the Holy Angels, Benilde–St. Margaret's, and Cretin-Derham Hall, where they work to preserve the schools' heritage and long-held values.

St. Joseph's Academy, the first school opened by our sisters upon their arrival in 1851 and Minnesota's oldest private school, closed in 1971, the 120th anniversary year of its founding. The painful decision brought a great deal of sorrow to both our province community and the broader St. Paul community. While sadness pervaded the school's last year, students and faculty considered that year to be the school's best. The alumnae association continues to be active and offers scholarships to young people seeking a Catholic education.

St. Anthony High School, a parish-owned school in Northeast Minneapolis, also closed in 1971. Lengthy discussions involving the parish, the Sisters of St. Joseph, and the archdiocese preceded the decision. While our sisters emphasized the need for a Catholic girls' high school east of the Mississippi River in Minneapolis, and despite successful efforts to increase the school's enrollment, factors such as the decreased number of sisters serving in the school and the parish's limited financial assets forced the decision. According to newspaper reports of the time, the Minnesota Legislature, faced with the closing of Catholic schools and the corresponding possible impact on public schools, began serious discussions to give financial aid to nonpublic schools.

Among the many sisters at the secondary level who were outstanding educators was Sister Mary Aloysius Sherin, or "Mary Al" as she was known to students and faculty. She spent forty-eight years as a teacher, counselor, registrar, and principal in Twin Cities area Catholic schools. As a teacher of math and science, she had a reputation for being strict. Years later, she told a Cretin-Derham Hall graduate that it was "all a put-on. I had to look stern so the students wouldn't take advantage of me." Sister Mary Al is still remembered today with great affection by her former students.

Sister Andre Nilles, who once described herself as "an endangered species" as a secondary school educator, developed social studies curriculum units that reflected worldwide social, cultural, and political systems. Her extensive travel through Europe and Asia helped broaden students' perspectives and appreciation of diversity. Some students from Derham Hall High School were traveling with Sister Andre in 1968 when Russia invaded Czechoslovakia, and together they felt the terror of political unrest.

The Sisters of St. Joseph were not as numerous as other religious communities in North Dakota, yet we made significant educational contributions in the state. Our educational work began in 1890 when we opened St. John's Academy, a boarding and day school in Jamestown. In 1963, the parish decided to close the high school. After the closing, Sister Rosanne Wanzek returned to the grade school to teach organ and piano. She had first learned piano at the school and considered it a privilege to minister to people in her hometown.

Grand Forks was the site of two grade schools, St. Mary's and St. Michael's, and one secondary school, the Academy of St. James, all staffed by the Sisters of St. Joseph for many decades. Sister Rose Mary Rooney taught first graders at St. Mary's for twenty-five years. The University of North Dakota, aware of her expertise in developing a student-centered classroom, involved her in the training of new teachers for many years.

North Dakota native Sister Frieda Kalenze served as superintendent of schools for the Bismarck Diocese in the 1980s. In her enthusiasm for the resurgence of interest in

Catholic school education, both locally and nationwide, she developed a long-range planning process for diocesan schools. After taking a tour with Frontiers of Justice to Mexico and El Salvador, Sister Frieda brought the message of poverty and hunger back to the young people of North Dakota and encouraged them to be alert to world events and to see what they might do to help others.

Nebraska and Wisconsin have been the sites for Sister Genevieve Schillo's work in educational administration. She served as superintendent of schools in the Omaha Archdiocese and is currently director of Faith Formation in the Superior Diocese.

Just about everyone in St. Paul knew the founder of Christ Child School for Exceptional Children, Sister Anna Marie Meyers. This former professor of speech at the College of St. Catherine, after becoming paralyzed in an automobile accident, taught children reading, spelling, and speech from her bed at St. Joseph's Hospital. In 1950, with philanthropic support from area families, she opened Christ Child School on Summit Avenue in St. Paul. Ten teachers, including Sister Anna Marie, welcomed seventy students, many with severe physical and learning disabilities. Enrollment grew over the years, but after Sister Anna Marie's death in 1975 the school closed.

Our sisters have also been involved in two residential education programs. At both the St. Paul Catholic Orphanage (1869–1953) and the Catholic Boys' Home in Minneapolis (1878–1960) our sisters provided an elementary school program for students in grades one through eight.

With challenges brought about by societal and church changes, our sisters began to work on new educational ventures. The growing number of adult immigrants in the Twin Cities area in the 1980s and 1990s inspired some sisters to establish centers of learning for adult immigrants. The Vineyard Literacy program began in 1990 in the Frogtown neighborhood of St. Paul, an area with a high Asian population. It remains affiliated with the Laos Family Community, which encourages immigrants to seek needed education. Another Vineyard is located at Carondelet Center on Randolph Avenue. Classes are offered in English proficiency and math and computer skills to immigrants from Africa, Europe, and Central and South America, as well as Asia. Two former elementary school teachers and principals, Sisters Mary Martin Nelson and St. Luke Copeland, direct the literacy centers and work with other sisters who teach classes.

Learning in Style in South Minneapolis also addresses the needs of new immigrants from as many twenty-two countries. Sisters Agnes Foley and Mary Clare Korb, both of whom have been teachers and school administrators, founded the program. To accommodate the needs of the immigrants, Learning in Style offers classes in basic education, English proficiency, pre-GED and GED preparation, and computer competency.

Sister Agnes Foley, cofounder of Learning in Style, enjoys a conversation in English with new immigrants.

Some teachers have moved from classrooms to entrepreneurial educational projects. Editorial Development Associates (EDA) has become a successful production company, Good Ground Press, whose staff members write, edit, design, and produce religious education materials for youth and adults. "Our publications help people wrestle with what the Word of God asks of them in the good ground of their lives," says Sister Joan Mitchell, who founded EDA in 1981. Sister Therese Sherlock joined Sister Joan the next year, bringing an expertise in children's literature. Good Ground staff members now write five lectionary-based periodicals for children from preschool to junior high. They also publish *SPIRIT* for teens and *Sunday by Sunday* for adults, along with a variety of other books and programs. Each week over half a million children, young people, and adults use a Good Ground Press publication in a school, parish, or small Christian community or in a Confirmation or RCIA (Ritual of Christian Initiation of Adults) program.

Focus on Theology is a comprehensive, adult approach to Christianity begun by Sisters Kathleen Foley and Peggy O'Leary, in collaboration with professors from the University of St. Thomas. The program aims to give adults the opportunity to renew elements of Catholic teaching and to enrich their spiritual and intellectual lives. The two-year program consists of twenty-six video presentations and a book of essays, prayers, and other resources. The Focus on Theology program encourages personal and communal growth through conversation and prayer. It now has nationwide sales.

Another entrepreneurial effort, Project One-Fifty (POF), provides workshops for teachers in the creative use of hands-on materials so children can learn at their own pace. Sisters Michele Murphy and Joan Mary Wadsworth began this work in 1986 and named it Project One-Fifty to commemorate the 150th anniversary in that year of our congregation's arrival in

Sister Michele Murphy conducts one of many Project One-Fifty workshops for teachers.

the United States. POF's first workshop was held on the screen porch of the sisters' home in St. Peter, Minnesota. Today, this ministry is located in our Administration Center.

The educational consultant ministry of Sisters Jean Wincek and Colleen O'Malley reflects our educational traditions of emphasizing experiential learning and Christian social principles. With their experience as teachers and administrators and their training as learning styles specialists, they ground teachers in an experiential learning model of curriculum development that respects the diversity of students' ways of learning. Their work has its roots in current research on whole-brain learning and educational kinesiology. In addition to teaching graduate courses for Saint Mary's University of Minnesota and the University of St. Thomas in St. Paul, they are called upon by schools throughout the United States to do staff development.

As a community, we have had a long history of involvement in education. Many of our sisters continue to teach but outside the walls of the classrooms in which they once served. To be true to our ministry in education we try to remain attuned to the needs of a world where knowledge, growing at an exponential rate, can be used to bring about a more just world.

11

Continuing Our Commitment to Higher Education

ALL OF THE TEACHING, health care, and social service ministries we have been engaged in over the years have been built on the foundation of the education we received. Nearly every sister of the province has a college education, and many have received graduate degrees from a variety of institutions. Our ministries have greatly benefited from our education.

The foresight of Mother Seraphine Ireland—in a time when the education of women was not generally valued or approved—led to the founding of the College of St. Catherine at the beginning of the twentieth century. The original emphasis on the core values of academic excellence, the Catholic tradition, and a commitment to social justice continues today at the college.

"Energize yourselves!" This frequent admonition of Sister Antonia McHugh, first dean and president of the college, rang in the ears of the sisters and students during the early days. Indeed the energy and commitment of those early sisters set the college on its way, and new energy still keeps the college going and flourishing. As this institution nears its 100th anniversary (1905–2005), the mission of St. Catherine's is driven by the same kind of enthusiasm that filled the early sisters at the college. The tenth president, Sister Andrea Lee, carries on this mission with an energy worthy of Sister Antonia herself.

Sister Andrea values the courageous foresight, spiritual leadership, and educational vision that brought the college into being and sustained it throughout its history.

The attention, hard work, and spirit of the sisters have made the campus a lively and hospitable place. Those working and studying at the college over the years, and visitors as well, have taken pleasure in the beauty of the campus and the hospitality of those they meet.

As with most colleges the faculty has been the continuity and strength of St. Catherine's from its beginning. Sister Antonia McHugh, recognizing the essential role of teaching, made sure that her early faculty had strong academic credentials. Her priority of sending sisters to the best graduate institutions, here and abroad, produced the first cadre of professors at the college, and the tradition continued when new generations of sisters were sent for doctoral studies and then assigned to teach at the college.

The sisters distinguished themselves in their fields and helped to give the college its reputation for academic excellence. Not only were these professors involved in their classrooms, giving devoted attention to the students, but they also produced scholarly work and provided leadership in professional organizations. Most sisters traveled during their sabbatical leaves of absence or led student groups to Europe and other continents. Some sisters used their sabbatical leaves to bring educational advantages to the underserved. Sister Teresita Judd, a professor of biology, taught anatomy and bacteriology in the nursing program at Harlem Hospital in New York in order to help the program with accreditation. Among those with an international reputation was Sister Marie Philip Haley. Her devoted promotion of French culture in her classes and during NDEA (National Defense Education Act) summer institutes, held both on the campus and in France, brought her high honors from the French government.

Before the college grew to be the sizable institution it is today, the sisters not only taught or worked on campus but also lived with resident students, served as campus ministers, advised student clubs, housecleaned, and even picked up the grounds before events such as commencement ceremonies.

When the number of residential students continued to increase, living space for the sisters became more limited. The sisters lived everywhere—in offices that were sometimes theirs but that were also used by other faculty members during the day, or in closets (with windows but limited space) attached to classrooms. As one lay faculty member once said, "Some families have skeletons in their closets, but I have a sister in the closet off my classroom."

Resident facilities to accommodate students have been added over the past fifty years, beginning with St. Joseph Hall, a combination student center and residence hall, then four-story St. Mary Hall. When crowding continued, the college had a one-year permit in 1967–68 for ten mobile homes to provide living space for students. Sister Seraphim Gibbons of the math department valiantly volunteered to live with the students in this unique arrangement. Stanton and Crandall Halls, named for two nineteenth-century female social activists, were opened the following year to meet residential needs. The Alberta and Georgia student apartment buildings, built later on the Fairview Avenue edge of the campus, were named respectively for Sister Alberta (Fides) Huber, a college president, and Sister Georgia Morrison, a long-time day prefect in Whitby Hall.

The college has been blessed with a succession of innovative presidents from 1951 to 2000. Sisters Antonine O'Brien (1949–55), Mary William Brady (1955–61), Mary Edward Healy (1961–64), and Alberta Huber (1964–79) were members of the St. Paul Province. Sister Catherine McNamee (1979–84) came to the college from the Albany (New York) Province. The first laywoman, Anita Pampusch, had been a Sister of St. Joseph for twenty-five years prior to becoming acting president (1984) and then president (1985–97). Another laywoman, Mary Broderick, who had been administrative liaison between the Minneapolis and St. Paul campuses of the college, served as acting president from 1997 to 1998. The current president of St. Catherine's, Sister Andrea Lee, is a member of the Sisters, Servants of the Immaculate Heart of Mary, a congregation whose charism is remarkably similar to that of the Sisters of St. Joseph. The history of the college, *More Than a Dream: Eighty-five Years of the College of St. Catherine* (Ryan and Wolkerstorfer) provides extensive coverage of all of the presidents up to 1992.

The presidents, faculty members, and students all felt the effects of the Second Vatican Council in the late 1960s and early 1970s. When the students demanded more relevant theology classes, the theology department responded to their requests. Under the leadership of Sister Rosalie Ryan the department incorporated the new emphasis on Scripture and contemporary theology as called for by the Council.

Because of the Second Vatican Council the lives of the sisters changed. When we moved from wearing religious habits to contemporary dress, the students insisted that their rigorous dress code also be relaxed. During those years some sisters who had served as prefects on the dormitory floors moved off campus to live in small houses in various neighborhoods. Other sisters remained committed to the ministry of living with students as well as to their ministry of teaching.

St. Catherine's was a student-centered college long before that concept was fashionable. The college administration and faculty have always put the students first, thereby aiming to be true to its roots by helping women "be all of which woman is capable"—strong, independent, competent, and caring. A re-

Sister Angela Schreiber of the education department at St. Catherine's teaches a course in children's literature to students.

cent leadership statement speaks of giving women "the confidence to succeed."

When the enrollment of traditional-age students declined because the nearby College of St. Thomas chose to admit women, St. Catherine's initiated two new programs to meet the growing needs of women for higher education. The Re-entry Adult Program (REAP) enabled women beyond traditional college age to take classes and earn degrees along with other students. Women with full-time jobs or heavy family responsibilities who were unable to attend the REAP program appreciated the opening of Weekend College a few years later. They welcomed the innovative weekend format, which was directed by Mary Alice Muellerleile and Sister Therese Sherlock. This new format challenged faculty members to creatively revise curricula and teaching methods. Enrollment grew rapidly in this program.

Interdisciplinary teaching has been valued at the college throughout its history. Today's "core courses" are the latest version of that concept. A course called "The Global Search for Justice" helps make visible the college's long-time concern for social justice. Some faculty members find opportunities for their students to work with the various ministries of the Sisters of St. Joseph and to have their students interview sisters for "The Reflective Woman," the beginning interdisciplinary core course required of all new students.

The number of lay faculty expanded to meet the growing student population. The peak number of sisters teaching at the college came in the 1960s and 1970s. During the 1970s the hiring process became more complex as the college became more diversified and legal requirements in hiring became more stringent. Consequently, several sisters of the province, after completing doctoral degrees, found no openings at St. Catherine's and took positions at other institutions of higher learning. According to Sister Katherine Egan, associate professor of education at the University of St. Thomas, these sisters have been able to spread the mission of the Sisters of St. Joseph to other institutions, including the University of St. Thomas in St. Paul, Saint Mary's University of Minnesota in Minneapolis, the College of St. Scholastica in Duluth, and Cardinal Stritch University in Milwaukee.

Sister Marie Herbert Seiter has worked at St. Thomas since 1978. She is currently associate director of both the Center for Economic Education and the Center for Senior Citizens Education. Programs in senior citizen education have expanded at both St. Thomas and St. Catherine's, with some of the sisters teaching in the programs and others taking the opportunity to continue their lifelong dedication to learning.

Lifelong learning is of great value to all of us. Our province has had a Board of Studies for some years, which funds study at all levels and also encourages older sisters to participate in Elderhostels and other opportunities for learning in the United States and abroad.

When she was seventy years of age and after many years of elementary and secondary teaching and administration, and service in the Peace Corps, Sister Isabella Ferrell served as an adjunct faculty member with Cardinal Stritch University in Milwaukee. She received the Samuel Cardinal Stritch award in 1998 for, among other qualities, her "vast and comprehensive" knowledge and her spirit of caring and compassion.

Upon completing eleven years as president of Mount St. Mary's College in Los Angeles, Sister Karen Kennelly was awarded the Carondelet Medal, that college's highest honor. Before going to Mount St. Mary's in 1989, Sister Karen had been a professor of history and academic dean at St. Catherine's and then director of the St. Paul Province. During her tenure as president, Mount St. Mary's grew significantly and became a leader in multicultural education. During her busy life as an administrator Sister Karen managed also to continue her scholarly work on the history of women religious.

Collaborating with other institutions has been the college's heritage as far back as Sister Antonia McHugh. Collaboration took a step forward in the 1950s when the college began cooperative efforts with the Hill Reference Library and other colleges in the Twin Cities. Early cooperation among these institutions led to Cooperating Libraries in Consortium, known on the campuses as CLIC, which for some years now has had a computerized catalog of the holdings of the libraries.

Intercollege cooperation also made possible Area Studies programs, with each college contributing faculty members to interdisciplinary courses in various cultural areas, including Russia, the Middle East, and the Far East. Not only did some professors have opportunities for global education, but they

Sisters who taught in the early days of educational television remember set-ting off for the studio in blue-tinted headdresses because their usual white caused too much glare under the strong studio lights. Sisters Mary William Brady (left) *and Mary Davida Wood are pictured here in a KTCA studio.*

were also able to teach in collaboration with their colleagues from the other campuses. In the 1960s when KTCA, the public television station in the Twin Cities, proposed televising college courses, Area Studies courses were among the first to be offered. Several other sister and lay faculty members in English, history, music, and other departments also taught in the early days of educational television.

The Area Studies experience led to an exchange of students between St. Catherine's and the College of St. Thomas and soon with Macalester College and Hamline University in St. Paul and Augsburg College in Minneapolis. From time to time various faculty members also taught on campuses other than their own. This exchange led to the development of the Associated Colleges of the Twin Cities, known as ACTC, which continues to promote intercollege cooperation.

In another kind of institutional cooperation the St. Paul Diocesan Teachers College, which had prepared sisters to teach in Catholic elementary schools since 1927, began affiliation with St. Catherine's in 1950 and became part of the college's education department in 1957 (Raiche, p. 46).

In a significant cooperative venture in 1986 the College of St. Catherine merged with St. Mary's Junior College in Minneapolis, an institution also founded and sponsored by the Sisters of St. Joseph. The two institutions became known as the College of St. Catherine–St. Paul and the College of St. Catherine–Minneapolis. St. Mary's Junior College (formerly St. Mary's School of Nursing) was founded by Sister Anne Joachim Moore in 1964. From the start it was known for its innovative health care and social service programs at the associate degree level. Sister Anne Joachim, recognized for her gift of calling forth creativity and loyalty in her colleagues, encouraged the lay and sister faculty/staff to develop programs to fill special needs in the health professions. From the beginning the great concern of the sisters at the junior college had been to make higher education accessible to economically and culturally diverse students, as well as persons with visual or hearing impairments. Graduates have successfully filled many of the health care needs in the Twin Cities and beyond. With all the advantages the merger brought to both campuses, progress was at first slow and uneasy, but the venture has proved to be beneficial for the growth and expansion of both campuses.

Faculty members and students at St. Catherine's have enjoyed an intellectually stimulating atmosphere, including a well-selected library. But by the 1960s a new library was needed to house the expanding collection, which, for lack of space,

Sister Anne Joachim Moore served as president of St. Mary's Junior College from its founding in 1964 to 1986.

was spread around in several campus buildings. Under the capable leadership of Sister Marie Inez Johnson, director of the library, sisters of the staff and the library science faculty planned a new library building. Funds came from $1 million that had accumulated from personal gifts sisters at the college had turned in to the community over many years. Many students, faculty members, and staff recall the excitement of the day in 1962 when they helped carry books from several parts of the campus to the new library building. The helpers, after depositing an armload of books on the designated shelves, were invited to pick up a brownie at the exit. Alumnae remember counting the loads of books they carried by the number of brownies they ate.

Although this library building has kept up-to-date with developing technologies, a new strategic plan for the college includes renovating and expanding to create a Learning Commons for the twenty-first century. This area will allow students and faculty to connect technologically with global resources and allow others worldwide to connect with the college. Space will be reconfigured so that students and faculty will be able to collaborate on projects. The St. Catherine's Learning Commons will function in ways women learn today and allow for technological richness.

St. Catherine's has always aimed to be a state-of-the-art institution. For this reason it has expanded its fund-raising over the years. Mother Antonia McHugh's early reliance on the "living endowment" provided by the sisters' contributed services needed to be supplemented by outside sources. One of the college's first major efforts at fund-raising resulted in a matching grant from the Ford Foundation in the early 1960s. The funds raised to match the grant were intended for debt retirement, lay faculty salaries, library acquisitions, financial aid for students, and other needs as determined by the college, including an auditorium large enough to accommodate concerts, lectures, plays, and commencement ceremonies and a fine arts complex to house the art, music, and theater departments. During this, the college's first capital campaign, leadership came from the business community with assistance from fund-raising volunteers. For the first time the college sought gifts beyond its alumnae. Catholic parishes were asked to contribute, and many responded with generous pledges.

The task of completing the Ford Foundation match on time and seeing to the building of the auditorium and the fine arts complex fell to Sister Alberta Huber after Sister Mary Edward Healy left the presidency to become provincial superior. The east end of the college campus took on a new look with the auditorium, named for I. A. O'Shaughnessy, one of the major donors, and the fine arts complex, named to honor Mother Antonia McHugh. The auditorium became a center of culture in the Twin Cities, with music performed by the Minnesota Orchestra, the St. Paul Chamber Orchestra, and other cultural groups.

Today, under the bold leadership of Sister Andrea Lee, president, the college has plans to launch a multimillion-dollar drive to make it possible for St. Catherine's to remain at the forefront of Catholic women's colleges. Sister Andrea asked the

St. Paul Province for an unrestricted gift in support of the college's future. After several months of prayer and discernment our community decided to give an unrestricted gift of $20 million to help launch the campaign. Simple living and the common sharing of resources, along with careful financial planning and prudent investments in a good economy, made this gift possible.

As St. Catherine's has grown in size and complexity, the number of laypersons on the faculty and staff has increased greatly, and many sisters have retired from the faculty. Yet we continue to play a significant role at the college. Sisters make up one-third of the membership of the board of trustees. Through all the changes the college tries to uphold the spirit of the Sisters of St. Joseph.

The college, moving toward an enrollment of 5,000, now offers, in addition to the traditional undergraduate program, two-year, weekend, and graduate programs in a variety of

Students standing near the altar of Our Lady of Victory Chapel get instructions from Sister Susan Hames, codirector of campus ministry, about their role as eucharistic ministers.

fields. Campus ministry has undergone a recent revitalization with two enthusiastic codirectors, Sisters Susan Hames and Catherine Steffens, along with twenty or more other sisters and consociates as campus ministry volunteers. These and other sisters, including some from Bethany Convent, have become prayer partners with students who wish to have a closer relationship with community members.

As St. Catherine's looks ahead to its next century we continue to feel a great responsibility for the ministry of higher education there. We believe that higher education is an act of social justice—a way of empowering women to live full lives.

12

Healing the Body and Spirit

Y OU FILL A NEED IN THE COMMUNITY." "I am grateful to all the volunteers, nurses, and doctors for the exceptional work they render to people who need this kind of health service." These words, written by patients at St. Mary's Health Clinics, reflect their feelings about our ongoing commitment to provide quality health care services wherever there is a need.

Since the arrival of the Sisters of St. Joseph in St. Paul, our sisters displayed competency and creativity as they responded to emerging needs. In founding, ministering in, supporting, and then relinquishing our hospitals, sisters involved in health care demonstrated resiliency and adaptability. They held reputable positions both within and outside our health care institutions. Sisters were not only religious leaders but also pioneers and innovators in their fields, frequently introducing new services and technologies. Quality of care in our hospitals met and often exceeded state and national accreditation standards.

With the exception of Lutheran deaconesses, until the mid-1960s Catholic sisters were the only women who owned, administered, and sponsored hospitals. Congregations of women religious such as ours, recognizing the right of everyone to have adequate health care, wanted to give gospel-oriented service to others, especially those in need.

But radical societal changes in the 1960s and the aftermath of the Second Vatican Council brought profound changes in our ministries, including health care. With some sisters leaving our religious community and others choosing ministries outside our sponsored institutions, fewer sisters were available to serve in hospitals. At the same time, competent and committed members of the laity emerged as leaders in our Catholic institutions to carry on the health care work we began in the 1850s.

The first hospital in the State of Minnesota, St. Joseph's in downtown St. Paul, had a reputation of being up-to-date, innovative, visionary, and dedicated to excellent patient care, as did St. Mary's in Minneapolis, at one time the largest hospital in the Twin Cities area. These same characteristics describe a long series of exceptionally capable sisters who led these two hospitals, among them Sister Marie de Paul Rochester at St.

Joseph's (1956–65 and 1968–77) and Sisters Rita Clare Brennan (1953–62) and Mary Madonna Ashton (1962–82) at St. Mary's. When speaking

Sister Mary Madonna Ashton, assistant administrator at St. Mary's Hospital in Minneapolis in 1959, wore a hard hat as she directed traffic during a Civil Defense hospital evacuation drill. Volunteers, who acted as patients, and 20 percent of the staff made the trip to emergency quarters in Mankato, Minnesota. (© 2000 STAR TRIBUNE/Minneapolis–St. Paul)

about what makes a good administrator, Sister Rita Clare once said, "She must keep on top of things in this rapidly changing field and should be flexible enough to roll with the changes. She needs to have a vision of what's going to happen and prepare for the future today."

Sisters collaborated with the hospital staff to develop programs and services that would continue Christ's healing mission by responding to the medical needs of patients. While St. Joseph's and St. Mary's Hospitals were similar in many ways, each made a unique contribution to the Catholic health care field. In the summer of 1914, a small group of sisters and other health care professionals, including Sisters Esperance Finn and Madeline Lyons and Jesuit Father Charles Moulinier, gathered on the back porch of St. Mary's Hospital to discuss how they might support one another in their ministry and speak with one voice on issues that impact health care. Out of this meeting grew the Catholic Health Association, which now has more than 2,000 member institutions. At its sixteenth annual convention in 1931, association officers placed a marker in the backyard of St. Mary's Hospital commemorating Sisters Esperance and Madeline as cofounders with Father Moulinier and naming St. Mary's Hospital as its birthplace.

As possibilities for new surgical procedures emerged in the late 1950s, surgeons needed a place to develop teams of special assistants to perform open-heart surgery. In response, long before animal rights was a societal issue, St. Joseph's Hospital opened an animal research laboratory. Sister Victorine Long, an experienced medical technologist, directed the laboratory and assisted with most procedures. Research ranged from implanting permanent pacemakers to developing intricate inner ear procedures. In 1959 doctors performed the first open-heart surgery in St. Paul at St. Joseph's. Cardiac surgeons at St. Mary's also did animal research under strict, sterile operating room conditions. Heart surgery and cardiac care became recognized specialties in both hospitals.

Family-centered maternity care—a welcoming, homelike atmosphere for parents and newborns—became a hallmark of both St. Joseph's and St. Mary's Hospitals. Initiated at St. Joseph's by Sister Mary Meyer, a highly respected maternity supervisor, the concept spread rapidly to other hospitals. During the mid-1960s, St. Mary's recorded approximately 400 deliveries a month, often broadcasting the arrival of the enviable "first New Year's baby" in the Twin Cities.

In our hospitals, patients and their families experience life-altering events such as the great joy of bringing a baby into the world or the deep sorrow of receiving a life-threatening diagnosis. Realizing that caring for the whole person by responding to spiritual needs could be as critical to health and well-being as giving good medical care, both St. Joseph's and St. Mary's established pastoral care departments. Along with our sisters, clergy, chaplains of other denominations, laypersons, and permanent deacons became integral components in the healing environments of our hospitals. In addition, each hospital developed a clinical pastoral education program to provide pastoral care and spiritual formation for future lay ministers and chaplains.

A chaplain at St. Joseph's Hospital, Sister Geri Lane, recalled a time when she found a teenage runaway sitting uncomfortably in a corner of his dying mother's room (*Challenge*, June 2000, p. 8). The boy told Sister Geri that he would like to talk to his mother but had no words. Quietly Sister Geri wrote, and invited the boy to consider, four possibilities of things to say: "I'm sorry," "Thank you," "I love you," and "Goodbye—I'll be OK." After twenty minutes alone with his mother, the boy came into the hallway and gave the rumpled paper to Sister Geri saying, "I said I am sorry, thank you, and I love you, but I couldn't say goodbye." Sister Geri affirmed his courage and assured him that

An ad for HealthEast Heart Care, which ran in the St. Paul Pioneer Press *from July through November 2000, confirms the commitment to healing both body and spirit. Through the ministry of hospital chaplains, patients and their families find, in the words of HealthEast, "sanctuary for the heart and soul."*

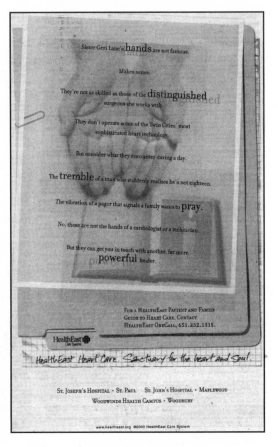

his mother had heard his words. Ninety minutes later, his mother died.

As with the pastoral care program, our sisters continued to recognize emerging needs and made plans to address them. St. Mary's Hospital developed the nationally renowned St. Mary's Chemical Dependency program, the first of its kind both in Minnesota and in a private acute care hospital in the upper Midwest. This unique program became known as the Minnesota Model, combining the medical approach with the Alcoholics Anonymous tradition.

Long-term care, physical medicine, and rehabilitation became rapidly developing medical specialties in the 1960s. Responding to the needs of convalescing and chronically ill patients, Sister Mary Madonna Ashton facilitated the opening of a Convalescent and Nursing Home at St. Mary's, later named the Rehabilitation Center, to provide the continuum of care frequently needed by these patients.

As new technologies and specializations flourished, the vision and pioneering spirit of our sisters and the hospital staffs at St. Joseph's and St. Mary's often provided patients with diagnostic and treatment options not available elsewhere in the area. The proliferation of programs and services designed to meet the needs of a growing patient population required major building programs, renovations, and restructuring of departments at both hospitals during the 1950s, 1960s, and 1970s. Educational programs and opportunities both within the hospitals and in collaboration with colleges, universities, and other health care providers became integral to patient care.

Sister Marie de Paul Rochester (center) was a leader in the province's health care ministry for forty-four years. For nineteen of those years she served as administrator at St. Joseph's Hospital, where she was often involved in building expansion projects to make the hospital an area leader in health care. She is pictured with two other staff members, Sisters Anne (Teresa Louise) McGuire (left) and Mary Meyer. (Russell Schweizer Photography, St. Paul)

This era of expansion also saw radical change in the governance of St. Mary's and St. Joseph's Hospitals when, by the early 1970s, a board of trustees composed of laity and sisters replaced the two existing boards—a lay advisory board and a board of sisters only. While the leadership of our province retained certain powers, such as appointment of the hospital administrator, the newly constituted board of trustees exercised responsibility for the direction and oversight of hospital operations. Another shift occurred as senior management positions, originally almost exclusively in the hands of sisters, became ministries open to the laity. Catholic hospitals across the United States experienced similar changes during the 1960s and 1970s.

Even more changes were on the horizon for our hospitals. Continuing scientific and medical discoveries produced new diagnostic equipment, surgical procedures, and medications that eventually contributed to a dramatic reduction in hospital admissions and lengths of stay. Hospitals responded to these developments in a variety of ways, including the consolidation of services within and among hospitals and the merger of major facilities.

Perhaps the most dramatic changes in health care began in 1965, when Medicare, the national health insurance program for persons sixty-five years of age and over, implemented cost containment procedures to ensure efficient delivery of health care services. The third-party determination of level of care and level of reimbursement for hospitals and physicians greatly affected their traditional roles. The emergence of health maintenance organizations further controlled medical practice by changing the focus from illness care to illness prevention. Decisions previously made by individual physicians gradually shifted to government and third-party payors. By the end of the 1970s, outside parties, including the government, were involved in the assessment and regulation of health care, ultimately controlling its destiny.

Explaining why anyone would stay in the field of hospital administration during times of such rapid change, Sister Mary Madonna Ashton, administrator at St. Mary's for twenty years, said, "It is important that Catholic hospitals continue Christ's healing mission, and that a religious community is present to carry out that mission. I am convinced that there is no better place to influence that mission than in the CEO position. This is an awesome responsibility as well as a great privilege."

Our Twin Cities hospitals, St. Joseph's and St. Mary's, saw this time of dramatic change in health care as an opportunity to explore the possibilities of closer cooperation. The hospital boards agreed to consolidate the two hospitals in 1985, calling the new entity Carondelet Community Hospitals with Carondelet LifeCare Corporation as the parent organization. Sister Karen Kennelly, then director of the St. Paul Province, described the consolidation as "one that will ensure a strong Catholic presence in the Twin Cities for years to come, while allowing St. Joseph's and St. Mary's to maintain their separate identities and serve their separate communities."

For many years St. Mary's Hospital worked cooperatively with its next-door neighbor, Fairview Hospital. Recognizing that closer affiliation could be advantageous to both hospitals, St. Mary's Hospital and Rehabilitation Center entered into a fifty-fifty joint venture with Fairview Health System in the late 1980s. Within two years, however, Carondelet LifeCare Corporation found that the amount of capital required to bring the site to the "state of the art" was prohibitive. Consequently, in 1991, Fairview offered to purchase St. Mary's, making it a health facility of Fairview Health System and renaming the two hospitals Riverside Medical Center. Although our decision to sell St. Mary's ended our role in a beloved institution, we looked to the future and began to investigate how we might meet the needs of people in the Minneapolis area who did not have access to traditional health care.

Meanwhile, pressure was building on St. Joseph's Hospital to enter into closer alignment with health care delivery in St. Paul. St. John's, a Lutheran hospital, together with Midway, a Baptist hospital, and Bethesda, another Lutheran hospital, were exploring ways in which they could cooperate. Board members became increasingly aware that hospitals with a religious mission needed to promote the religious and ethical values on which they were founded. In 1987 our province leaders approved the incorporation of St. Joseph's into the HealthEast System, retaining certain reserved powers to ensure its continuing catholicity.

Many St. Paul residents received with dismay the news announcement in August 1996 that St. Joseph's Hospital would relocate from downtown St. Paul to Woodbury, a rapidly expanding suburb of the Twin Cities. However, within a year HealthEast reversed its decision to close the downtown hospital, convinced by concerned physicians, employees, St. Paul citizens, and others that the increasing patient census and growing needs of the downtown St. Paul community warranted retaining a hospital there. Reflecting on her many years as administrator at St. Joseph's Hospital, Sister Marie de Paul Rochester affirmed the HealthEast decision saying, "We are part of a long tradition, a great heritage of service to the St. Paul community. To be part of St. Joseph's Hospital, the oldest in Minnesota, inspires one with a sense of [pride in] both civic and religious communities."

The Woodwinds Health Campus in Woodbury, a full-service health facility, opened its doors in 2000. The environment of the new campus, shaped by the belief that healing comes from within the person, incorporates complementary healing therapies with traditional medical practices. The seventy-bed St. Joseph's Hospital on the Woodwinds campus is, in addition to downtown St. Joseph's Hospital, sponsored by our province and continues our tradition of providing health care services that respond to local needs.

While the Twin Cities' health care environment in the 1980s and 1990s prompted our province and hospital leaders to talk with nearby hospitals and health care groups regarding the future of our institutions, our congregational leaders were envisioning a congregation-wide plan for addressing the needs of the times. The congregational planning resulted first in the formation of a network of loosely affiliated hospitals sponsored by the Sisters of St. Joseph of Carondelet in 1981 and then in the development of a full system, Carondelet Health System, in 1986. In the system's early years, St. Mary's and St. Joseph's Hospitals as well as St. John's Hospital in Fargo were members, Sister Marie de Paul Rochester was the first chair of the board, and Sister Mary Heinen was executive director and later vice president for mission.

But the growing complexity of health care programs and services in the Twin Cities and in the upper Midwest resulted in major changes in the relationship between our hospitals in the St. Paul Province and the congregational system. After we sold St. Mary's and St. John's, and St. Joseph's became an integrated unit of HealthEast, and after a multiyear process of dialogue with Carondelet Health System representatives, our congregational leaders, and the sisters in our province, the St. Paul Province withdrew from the Carondelet System. At the same time, our congregation's other three provinces recommitted themselves to strengthening the system. Although our withdrawal from the system created controversy and raised questions from our congregational leadership and the other provinces, the sisters in the St. Paul Province supported the decision.

For over 100 years, our sisters' commitment to health care has included providing professional nursing education. By the mid-1890s both St. Mary's and St. Joseph's Hospitals had opened nursing schools. After the College of St. Catherine began awarding a baccalaureate degree in nursing in 1942, the two hospitals arranged to have their students take science and beginning nursing courses at the college and receive three-year nursing diplomas from St. Catherine's. Sister Agnes Leon Mahowald, director of St. Catherine's nursing program for nine years beginning in 1947, recalls the challenge of helping the three-year students, who lived at the hospitals, feel part of the college community. With Sister Agnes Leon's leadership, the nursing program received accreditation from the National League for Nursing.

Following Sister Agnes Leon, Sister Mary Jane Linn worked tirelessly for twenty-six years as director of the nursing department. Continuing what her predecessors began, she developed a strong, innovative collegiate nursing program. Recognized by her colleagues as ahead of her time in her belief that nursing education belonged in a baccalaureate setting, her work had an impact on nursing education throughout the United States.

After the 1960s the College of St. Catherine offered only a four-year nursing program using St. Joseph's Hospital for clinical experience while St. Mary's Hospital retained the three-year nursing diploma program. With the founding of St. Mary's Junior College by Sister Anne Joachim Moore in 1964, the nursing program became a two-year associate degree. The junior college developed several additional health care–related associate degree programs as the need for specially prepared professionals and technicians grew. When St. Mary's Junior College and the College of St. Catherine merged in 1986, the two institutions brought together their traditions of educating well-prepared professionals to serve in the health care field.

Like our Twin Cities hospitals, our three North Dakota hospitals, founded between 1900 and 1917 at the invitation of local business leaders and doctors, faced the challenges of a rapidly changing health care environment. Each hospital, St. Michael's in Grand Forks, St. John's in Fargo, and Trinity in Jamestown, engaged in major building programs to accommodate services that were, in some cases, the first in the State of North Dakota. Noted for their cardiac surgery, birthing rooms, and circular patient care formats, as well as their extended care and chemical dependency units, the hospitals demonstrated the future-oriented stance of our sisters and the staffs of the hospitals. Sisters collaborated with lay colleagues in private and community hospitals and in state universities as they developed our health care ministry in response to local needs.

Working in hospitals in North Dakota brought unique challenges for our sisters, especially when the natural elements interrupted daily routines. Blizzards and "snirt" (snow and dirt) storms sometimes kept hospital personnel at work far beyond regular shifts. Visitors and even patients would offer their assistance. Frequent spring flooding from the Red River caused significant disruption of services at St. John's Hospital. When Sister Vernard Blanz became administrator in 1953, she faced the problem of convincing local officials to authorize a flood control program for the area. As a result of Sister Vernard's skillful negotiation with civic leaders, the Army Corps of Engineers straightened the curve of the river to prevent ice jams. They also built an earthen dike to prevent floodwaters from reaching the hospital and the major business area of Fargo.

Local citizens and city leaders valued our health care ministry in their communities. When, in 1962, we announced that St. John's Hospital would close because of the competition of two other medical groups in Fargo, the mayor and city council formed a "Save St. John's Committee." Their initiative resulted in the reversal of the decision. However, in 1985 we sold St. John's to the Franciscan Sisters of Little Falls, Minnesota, who operated another hospital nearby, thus leaving a Catholic health care presence in the area.

In Grand Forks our hospital underwent changes similar to those in other health care institutions, first building, then merging. A citywide campaign in 1951 raised funds for a new $4-million, 200-bed hospital to replace the "old" St. Michael's structure built in 1907. The old St. Michael's became St. Anne's Home and served as a long-term care facility. Eventually St. Michael's merged with Deaconess Hospital to become

Sister Carol Neuburger, in the white habit, and other hospital personnel gathered the children in the pediatric department at St. Michael's Hospital in Grand Forks, North Dakota, for a visit from the Shriners, dressed as clowns. Sister Carol's nursing ministry included visiting children who were dying of cancer in their homes.

part of United Hospital affiliated with the University of North Dakota.

The transformation of Trinity, our hospital in Jamestown, took a different path. When Sister Brigida Cassady arrived in Jamestown in 1965, her charge was to transfer our hospital to the city of Jamestown. On the day of the public announcement, local newspaper headlines read: "Unique Experiment Has Paid Rich Dividends for Jamestown Hospital." The report continued: "Take some Roman Catholic nuns, mix them with laypeople of all denominations, combine all the ingredients in a Lutheran-sponsored hospital, stir—and hope." Calling it a successful and advantageous health plan, Sister Brigida stressed that "it didn't just happen." She emphasized that Trinity Hospital was not forced to close, nor was Jamestown Hospital forced to merge, and explained that "sharing hospital facilities today is gaining nationwide consideration that was not so evident three years ago when this plan was conceived." Four sisters who wanted to stay in Jamestown applied for and received positions at the Jamestown Hospital.

The education of professional nurses in North Dakota was as important to the delivery of health care to patients there as in our in Twin Cities hospitals. Thus, between 1901 and 1915 we opened schools of nursing in the North Dakota cities where we had hospitals. The history of these three schools of nursing provides another example of how our sisters in health care ministry responded to the needs of the time.

Seeing an opportunity to strengthen the curricula of our three schools and to offer university credits for courses, in 1947 Sister Enid Collins amalgamated the three independent units to form the Sisters of St. Joseph School of Nursing of North Dakota in Grand Forks. Five years later our nursing school arranged a closer alliance with the University of North Dakota College of Nursing. By the late 1960s plans were underway to phase out the nursing school and to transfer the students to an associate degree in nursing program, directed by Sister Mary Heinen, at North Dakota State University in Fargo. By the mid-1980s the program merged into a bachelor of science degree.

Although we no longer minister in health care in North Dakota, many of the institutions and programs we founded have been transformed to respond to local needs. Competent and dedicated laypersons now carry on the work we began.

When the Sisters of St. Joseph of Superior, Wisconsin, merged with the St. Paul Province in 1986, their hospital, Holy Family in New Richmond, Wisconsin, became a welcome addition to the health care ministry of our province. Since the sisters from Superior founded Holy Family Hospital in 1949, it has served the New Richmond community and west central Wisconsin by providing a wide range of services. Sister Marian Schmit, who has worked at the hospital over forty years, has seen it undergo several remodeling projects to accommodate growing health care needs. Sister Marian brought her love of being with people to her diverse ministries of nurse, X-ray technologist, patient representative, and pastoral care worker. "I always get back more than I've given," she says.

As networking became increasingly important to providing quality health care services, Holy Family continued to shape its vision for the future. In collaboration with the city of New Richmond, the hospital added medical helicopter transport to its services in the late 1980s. During the 1990s Holy Family expanded its services in conjunction with area hospitals to create the Heartland Home Care Network, and in 1999, in partnership with Presbyterian Homes and Services, senior housing and assisted living facilities were constructed on the Holy Family Campus. Also in 1999, an affiliation agreement with Health Partners, a Minnesota-based health maintenance organization, added strength to our hospital's future vision. Holy Family undertook a $13-million development program that included construction of the New Richmond Physicians Clinic on the campus and a completely redesigned hospital.

It is no coincidence that the major expansion plan followed closely upon Holy Family's anniversary, which celebrated "building on fifty years of care." Reflecting on the hospital's history, Holy Family's president, Jean Needham, noted: "It is because of the splendid cooperation of families and individuals in this area that Holy Family Hospital has attained its present-day status. The dream of the few became the successful venture of the many."

Our commitment to providing health care services began a new phase when, in the 1980s, Sisters Brigida Cassady and Jean Hare became aware of emerging needs in the Twin Cities area. They observed trends such as a shortage of well-prepared home care personnel and a growing population of poor elderly

persons. In response to the situation, they developed Sisters Care. Beginning in 1987, this program connected sisters who had retired from

As early as 1969, Sister Brigida Cassady worked out of a store-front on Franklin Avenue in Minneapolis. She provided basic necessities to people who were not apt to approach social service agencies and connected them with such agencies when their problems required it. With Sister Jean Hare, Sister Brigida is cofounder of Sisters Care.

other ministries with persons who were frail or elderly, had limited financial resources, and wished to remain in their own homes.

Sisters from six different religious communities work as caregivers for Sisters Care. After taking a certified home health aide class, they begin their ministry of giving personal care and homemaking assistance to persons who apply for their services. Often strong personal bonds develop between the client and caregiver, since the same sister sees the person at each visit. At times clients say to caregivers, "Sister, don't clean anything today. Just sit and talk to me."

"We want our clients to experience quality of life in their own homes for as long as possible. That is part of our mission," explains Sister Frances Mary Benz, current codirector with Sister Donna Sklar. "Loneliness is a big problem for persons who are frail or have a disability. We ask our caregivers to encourage clients to socialize with others as much as they are able, so they don't feel so isolated," she said. In 1990 the Catholic Health Association recognized Sisters Care at a national convention in Washington, D.C., by presenting this ministry with its achievement award, an honor usually given to acute care programs and facilities.

With the sale of St. Mary's Hospital to the Fairview Health System in 1991, we resolved to apply nearly 150 years of health care experience to a disturbing problem. Many thousands of Twin Cities' residents were without medical care because they could not afford health insurance and did not qualify for subsidized government health care programs. After twenty years of ministry in acute health care administration, eight years as Commissioner of Health for the State of Minnesota, and with initial experience as a medical social worker, Sister Mary Madonna Ashton developed a plan to care for this underserved population in the greater Twin Cities area.

The first St. Mary's Health Clinic opened in January 1992, and by 2000 eleven free, nondenominational clinics were in operation: two in Minneapolis, four in St. Paul, and five in suburban areas. The clinics occupy donated space in existing facilities such as schools, community centers, and churches. These health clinics provide primary care services, including health screenings and education as well as treatment of numerous acute and chronic conditions, averaging 4,500 patient visits per year.

A core group of staff members oversees clinic operations. In addition, more than 200 volunteer physicians, nurses, admissions personnel, interpreters, and drivers serve the clinics, and 800 specialty physicians see patients in their offices without charge when referred by a clinic physician. Health care services at our clinics are coordinated with other community agencies, and collaborative arrangements exist with area hospitals, laboratories, and pharmacies.

Another of our health services, massage therapy, began in the 1970s. While caring for her ailing mother in North Dakota, Sister Rosalind Gefre, a licensed practical nurse, experienced firsthand how massage relieved severe pain. After receiving training, she began doing her ministry of massage therapy, with "Christ's healing touch" as the center of her mission. When she came from North Dakota to Minnesota in 1983 to establish a therapeutic massage center in St. Paul, she learned that the requirements included fingerprinting, a mug shot, and a $500 annual license fee. At a city council meeting she explained that therapeutic massage is legitimate health care and nothing else. As a result, the required fingerprinting and mug shot were eliminated, and the license fee was reduced to $50. Sister Rosalind has opened four massage schools—in St. Paul, Mankato, Rochester, and Fargo, plus four clinics in the Twin Cities area where students from her schools do their

Our ministry in Jonestown, Mississippi, one of the poorest areas of the United States, began when Sisters Agatha Grossman (left), Victorine Long, and Manette Durand opened a health clinic for people long deprived of such care.

practicum work. Since Sister Rosalind's pioneering spirit brought legitimacy to the field of massage, other sisters have been educated to work in this ministry.

One of our health care ministries that began near the North Dakota border now takes place far beyond the upper Midwest area. In the late 1960s, Sisters Mary Nicholas Vincelli and Patricia DeBlieck, both registered nurses, provided health services for migrant workers who harvested beets in the Red River Valley every summer. After a few years Sister Mary Nicholas moved to Texas, where most of the migrants she knew lived. Seeing the great need for a certified nurse-midwife to upgrade the quality of prenatal care, she successfully recruited Sister Patricia, who had been working as a midwife in Mississippi, to come to Hidalgo County in Texas. Both sisters have received statewide recognition in Texas for their outstanding service of bringing health care services to the area, especially to women who experience high-risk pregnancies.

In the early 1990s, Sister Manette Durand, a nurse practitioner, along with Sisters Agatha Grossman, a nurse, and Victorine Long, a medical technologist, reached out in another direction by establishing a clinic for the economically poor in

Over the years, other sisters joined our sisters serving in the health care ministry in Jonestown, Mississippi, and helped establish a learning center. Sister Patricia DeMoully (center) later became coordinator of a nearby Habitat for Humanity project. Although Sister Pat never became a professional homebuilder, she readily talked about "laying a slab floor, handling a cutoff saw, and wiring a building."

Jonestown, Mississippi. In this town of 1,500 residents, 98 percent are African American women and men who have little or no opportunity for permanent jobs. The clinic gives primary care, including physical examinations, laboratory tests, and education on nutrition and parenting to approximately sixty men, women, and children each week.

As health care became more complex, we, along with others, recognized the importance of sponsoring an ethics center. In 1989 the College of St. Catherine and Riverside Medical Center jointly created an ecumenical center for excellence in medical and health care ethics. By 1992 the Minnesota Center for Health Care Ethics broadened its membership to include

HealthEast and the St. Paul Province of the Sisters of St. Joseph. The center's work includes providing health care ethics consultation and educational programs for its sponsors. The center's director, Karen Gervais, has a national reputation as a perceptive and thoughtful ethicist.

Our sisters who have worked in health care have seen their ministry as a way to heal the body and the spirit. Sister Marie de Paul Rochester's words, describing the work of a hospital, could apply to all our health care ministries: "A hospital is a place where life's most profound questions are asked. Frequently they are questions that have no answer, for which faith in what we believe and what we can become, is the only answer. It is the people who make up the hospital who witness to its philosophy, to the infinite value and deep mystery of each human person, to the uniqueness of each patient and coworker." It is in this spirit that we continue our work of responding to the health care needs of the times.

13

Developing Pastoral and Spirituality Ministries

THE SECOND VATICAN COUNCIL made official what many theologians were already teaching—that all persons, not
just ordained clergy, were called to proclaim the good
news of Jesus Christ. For Sisters of St. Joseph that meant we
could involve ourselves more directly in the work of the church
through pastoral and spirituality ministries.

Sisters began to work in parishes, on college and university campuses, and in hospitals doing whatever was needed to
enrich the lives of those we served. Graduate programs in theology and training in pastoral ministries opened up for women,
and many of us took advantage of these opportunities. St.
Mary's College in South Bend, Indiana, led the way with graduate programs in theology for women. By the late 1960s major
Catholic universities began to admit women for graduate study
in theology departments formerly limited to men.

Some sisters eagerly entered this new world and began to
study at graduate schools of theology such as those at Notre
Dame, Marquette, and St. John's in Collegeville, Minnesota.
The College of St. Catherine began offering an undergraduate
major in theology and later a master's degree. In addition, the
theology department now offers certificate programs in spiritual direction and in pastoral ministry.

Pastoral ministry, earlier viewed by the church as an
extension of the hierarchy, had now become service given to the

people of the parish and the diocese by the nonordained. Sister Betty Ann Gits, the first pastoral minister from our province, was assigned in 1967 to a parish in the Archdiocese of St. Paul and Minneapolis. Upon hiring her the pastor said, "This is a very new thing; it's a kind of experiment. We're the only parish I know of that is doing anything like this. A woman can relate to women in the homes and reach people whom it is difficult for a priest to reach. You will begin by taking the parish census, visiting the sick, and working with young people."

Since then many of our sisters have served in pastoral ministries in Wisconsin, North Dakota, and other states as well as in Minnesota. They have been in both cities and rural areas in various roles: pastoral associate, pastoral minister, pastoral administrator, parish visitor, parish liturgist. Sisters have provided instruction for children preparing for First Communion and for adults in the process of Christian initiation. Pastoral workers have helped couples with marriage preparation and families with wakes, funerals, and graveside prayers at the time of the death of a family member. Often preparation of lectors, eucharistic ministers, and greeters is the responsibility of pastoral ministers. They also preside at Communion services and give scriptural reflections. Faith formation involves organizing programs for all age groups, including days of recollection and Lent and Advent series. Ministry to the sick and homebound brings help and the services they need to this population.

Sisters Caroline Pfeifer and Monica (Mary Helen) Frederick, both reared in the Twin Cities, took on all these responsibilities in Saxon, a small town in rural northern Wisconsin. For fourteen years they worked as a team to assist the pastor, who is assigned to four parishes in four different towns. Sister Caroline now continues the work alone because Sister Monica has retired. One of their many contributions was organizing a garage sale to raise funds for a ramp entrance to

Sisters Caroline Pfeifer (left) and Monica Frederick setting out from Saxon, Wisconsin, to minister at one of the other parishes they served. (Superior Catholic Herald)

the church in Saxon so elderly parishioners could again attend Mass and other services.

As pastoral ministers, sisters represent the care and concern of the church for many people. They try to respond to the needs of people who are troubled, hungry, homeless, or addicted. These increasingly include immigrants, prisoners, and those in need of advocates in court.

Pastoral care in hospitals, which has been a concern of our sisters serving in health care, became a separate department in these institutions. Sisters and others were required to have professional preparation and certification through completion of a program in clinical pastoral care before being appointed to staff positions. After receiving certification at Fairview Hospital in Minneapolis, Sister Angelica Carline was appointed chaplain assistant at St. Joseph's Hospital in St. Paul. The *St. Paul Dispatch* (January 3, 1973) referred to her position: "The idea of using women religious in pastoral service is gaining ground, but still is unusual. She is the first nun to be named to such a position in this area." Since that time, a number of our sisters have earned pastoral care certification and have held hospital positions.

The following year, Sister Rosanne Fox initiated the St. Olaf Outreach program at St. Olaf Church in downtown Minneapolis. Nearly three decades later, she and several sisters continue to promote the program's mission "to make Christ's presence visible to various groups of people in the city, the inner city, and the suburbs." After completing a master's degree in pastoral ministry at Seattle University in 1978, Sister Mary Hasbrouck joined the staff at St. Olaf, where she could put into practice her thesis subject, "Growth Toward Christian Adulthood," one of five critical issues identified in 1977 by the Regional Consultants for Adult Formation of the U.S. Catholic Conference.

Administration of a parish became the next step for some sisters. Bishop Raymond Lucker of the diocese of New Ulm, Minnesota, was among the first bishops in the United States to appoint pastoral administrators. The sisters who worked with him found him to be a man of vision who affirmed them in their ministries. He has said, "Granted there is a priest shortage, but it's also a question of recognizing people called and gifted by the Spirit. Every member of the church is gifted and called to ministry in some way." In 1982, Sister Marie Grossman moved

Sister Mary Lamski (center), who has worked in a variety of pastoral ministries, confers here with parishioners.

into her first year of internship and became the third woman religious to hold the position of pastoral administrator in the New Ulm Diocese. She served in this position for ten years, the usual term for a pastor.

As pastoral ministers, we experienced sadness with others in their loss and pain. But there was also a lighter side to these ministries. After arriving at the coal mining town of Big Stone Gap in Virginia, Sisters Julie Noonan and Julitta Walsh were greeted by "Doc," the pastor of the church there. Doc, so called because he had been a medic in World War II, surprised them by saying he was from St. Paul. Instantly they became friends. That night in the house-church every bed was spoken for. Where to put Sisters Julie and Julitta was solved with a cot set up in a storeroom and a mattress on the floor in the reconciliation room.

With a growing number of students in the public schools, some of our sisters answered the call to be directors and cate-chists in parish religious education programs. They worked with the particular needs of parents and children in coopera-tion wih clergy and staff at each parish. They helped develop programs in youth ministry and family-based catechesis, retreats, and sacramental programs.

In the 1970s and 1980s sisters enlarged their leadership efforts in religious education by traveling to rural, suburban, and city parishes to share their experiences with those working in existing programs, and they also initiated new programs. They planned conventions, offered workshops to small groups, and worked with individuals. By the end of the 1990s laypeo-ple sustained almost all religious education programs, and sis-ters had moved from dealing directly with students in class-rooms to teaching and preparing teachers, thus passing on their expertise.

Sister Mary Daniel Hartnett was the first woman to be hired for a full-time faculty position at the St. Paul Seminary.

A well-known educator in the archdiocese, she commented about her work, "To work each day with a faculty and students whose main goal is to struggle to unravel the mystery of God for themselves and others is a great privilege."

While pastoral ministry continues to grow, some sisters are now involved in spirituality ministry. Although we have always been spiritual companions who listened to people voicing their spiritual concerns, some sisters began to prepare themselves professionally for ministries in spiritual direction and for conducting retreats and days of prayer.

As a congregation we came to acknowledge spirituality as a community ministry. By the 1970s our congregation saw the appropriateness of establishing houses of prayer. A core community of sisters, who had previously been involved in other works, opened our House of Prayer in Stillwater, Minnesota. This peaceful place became a respite for many sisters as well as for our friends among the laity. The core members created an atmosphere of beauty and peace in a building that had originally been a parish convent. Sisters Mary Mark Mahoney and Rose Carmel Engesser remained with what came to be called Still Water for its fifteen-year existence. They and the other sisters of the core community made hospitality a real ministry and offered spiritual direction to those who wished it.

As more and more sisters engaged in a variety of spirituality ministries, Sisters Mary Margaret Deeney and Margaret Kvasnicka initiated a spirituality network to give support and encouragement to members of the province working in these ministries. At the regular potluck supper meetings members share ideas about financing and marketing their entrepreneurial ministries. More importantly, they share spiritual nourishment and talk about ways their ministries fulfill our province's mission. One of the network's projects was a province-wide study of the feasibility of starting a new house of prayer to replace the one in Stillwater. Sisters showed sufficient interest in using such a facility but not in staffing it. Network members gave full support, however, to the province's reimagining the uses of Carondelet Center, formerly the novitiate building, which now houses offices of several of our spirituality ministries.

Until she became a member of the province leadership in 1994, Sister Margaret Kvasnicka, with another spiritual director, offered Transitions, a ministry to help women discern new directions for their lives. Sister Margaret returned to Carondelet Center in 2000 to continue her ministry of what she now calls "Exploring the Intersections: Justice, Spirituality, Mission."

"Journey: Spiritual Growth Opportunities" grew out of Sister Mary Margaret Deeney's experience in teaching and in formation ministry for the province. After earning a graduate degree in theology, she established a ministry to meet the needs of those seeking companionship in their spiritual journey. For years she has given spiritual direction in her office in Carondelet Center and continues to lead retreats and days of reflection in parishes in the Twin Cities and suburbs. One of her specialties is helping individuals and groups learn more about themselves through the Enneagram, a method of self-inventory that allows for deeper understanding of self and one's relationship with others.

We say that Sisters of St. Joseph never retire; they only refocus. Sisters Eleanor Lincoln and Catherine Litecky, who retired after forty-five years of teaching at the College of St. Catherine, began a ministry they named Women at the Well. This ministry of theological and spiritual enrichment grew out of their experience in helping women in their classes gain greater insight into who they were. They give retreats in parishes encouraging women to live their everyday spirituality by

This logo for Women at the Well ministry, designed by Sister Joanne Emmer, represents Jesus speaking with women.

being at home with themselves, other people, creation, and God. They also offer online retreats.

The office of Women at the Well is located next to the Wisdom Ways Resource Center for Spirituality in Carondelet Center. Wisdom Ways, a collaborative venture of the St. Paul Province and the College of St. Catherine, provides a network of resources for spirituality in contemporary life and culture. All spiritual seekers, whatever their religious affiliations, find opportunities for theological education and spiritual growth. Mary Kaye Medinger, a consociate of the Sisters of St. Joseph and the founding director of Wisdom Ways, brought to this ministry her experience both as a pastoral minister and as coordinator of formation for the Permanent Diaconate Training program for the archdiocese. Her acquaintance with many persons involved in church ministry and renewal has allowed her to tap a wide range of expertise in offering programs. Annual summer spirituality institutes have drawn varied crowds from the United States and beyond. Prayer in many forms, music, art, dance, celebrating seasons and life stages, sharing hospitality, praising God as Holy Wisdom—all these are ways participants satisfy their hunger for spirituality. Many people prayerfully walk the Wisdom Ways labyrinth mowed into the lawn behind Carondelet Center.

Other spiritual directors working out of Carondelet Center include Sister Christine Loegering, who comes several days a month from the Dwelling in the Woods, located a hun-

Sisters walk the labyrinth maintained by Wisdom Ways on the Provincial House grounds.

dred miles north of the Twin Cities. The Dwelling, founded by Sister Christine and Sister Jeanne Stodola, aims to express the ageless wisdom that is at the heart of all great religions. Guests, who live in small hermitages or camp on the grounds, spend time in solitude. They may opt for spiritual direction, therapeutic massage, or yoga therapy.

Other sisters minister in a variety of spiritual direction settings throughout the area. One is Sister Mary Lamski, who also teaches in a program at the St. Paul Seminary. The Center for Spiritual Guidance, founded in 1990 by Sister Roseann Giguere and two other spiritual directors, has met for the past five years at Carondelet Center to prepare people to become spiritual directors. Sister Roseann earned a master of divinity degree from United Theological Seminary in St. Paul after working in prison ministry for several years.

Since 1976, our sisters have served at the Loyola spirituality resource center, founded by a Jesuit in St. Paul in that year. Sister Helen Dolores Sweeney was the first administrator and served until her death in 1986. One of the most active members of the province's spirituality network, Sister Elizabeth Kerwin, is currently director of Loyola, which, while principally serving men and women in the Twin Cities, has reached as far as Guatemala and Uganda.

As our first sisters met the spiritual as well as the physical needs of the people of their day, so do we try to respond to the spiritual needs of the people of God today.

14

Responding to Societal Needs

T HE STORY OF SISTER RITA STEINHAGEN reflects the evolution of many sisters from institutionally based ministries to direct social services and then to social justice issues and political action. As Sister Rita explains, "One thing led to another." After illness demanded she leave her work as a medical technologist, Sister Rita opened a Free Store on the West Bank in Minneapolis, a place where people could "shop" for what they needed. She became acquainted with many people, including runaway youth who spent their days and nights on the streets. One day a youth asked her, "Why don't you get us a place to stay?" So Sister Rita founded the Bridge, a shelter for runaway youth, not far from the Free Store.

"I was learning about the oppressive and unjust systems—what it is like to be poor with a constant struggle just to survive," recalls Sister Rita. Because many of the people she met spoke Spanish, "I decided it was time to learn that language. So I went to a small language school in El Paso, Texas, and worked at a nearby shelter for refugees. It was there that I first learned about the School of the Americas." After hearing the refugees' stories, Sister Rita went to Central America as a Witness for Peace and lived in the war zones in northern Nicaragua.

When she returned home, Sister Rita worked for seven years at the Center for Victims of Torture. Haunted by her experience of seeing the results of torture and by her knowledge of

U.S. complicity in training Latin American soldiers in methods of torture, she went to Fort Benning, Georgia, to participate in demonstrations opposing the School of the Americas. Because she "crossed the line a second time," a judge sentenced her to six months in federal prison, where "I got a crash course in our prison system and the unfairness of it all." Now, besides continuing to work to close the School of the Americas, she is involved with changing prison policies that are especially harsh on women with children.

Like Sister Rita, many sisters have become active in social justice movements. With the growing understanding in the 1960s that our religious vow of obedience meant much more than listening to the directives of our superiors and included being open to the Spirit by listening to the people and events of our times, we felt called to confront injustices wherever we saw them.

Sisters Kate McDonald (left), Marguerite Corcoran, and Brigid McDonald surround Sister Rita Steinhagen, who carries a cross commemorating one of numerous victims of soldiers trained at the School of the Americas in Fort Benning, Georgia.

Like our first sisters in France we continue to give direct service to those in need and work for systemic change. Sister Florence Steichen uses the phrase "walking on the two feet of justice," a metaphor developed in the 1970s to describe this dual task. Our stories from the past fifty years show how leadership has emerged whenever sisters have seen needs and responded to them.

Sisters, of course, have been responding to needs all along. Sister Lillian Meyer went to political caucuses in the early 1950s, subscribed to the *Congressional Record*, and vigorously contributed her knowledge and opinions in Saturday classes on current affairs she took at the College of St. Catherine. In the 1940s and 1950s Sister Julienne Foley taught Mexican children and adults. Downtown St. Paul merchants and cab drivers recognized her resolute gait as she fearlessly approached them for food and clothing for "her people" or asked for free rides. Throughout the years sisters visited students and families in their homes and provided clothing and other necessities. They also visited those who were poor and elderly at the Ramsey County "poor farm," in hospitals, and in prisons, as our earliest members had done.

Some of our sisters worked at the Catholic Infant Home, a residence program for pregnant girls. The sisters provided child care and personal and spiritual enrichment classes for the girls, while other organizations provided health care services. As attitudes toward single pregnant women changed, so did the program. This ministry, now called Seton Center, is no longer a residence and offers a variety of services for single parents and married couples.

As social issues and reform movements surfaced in the 1960s, our community experienced transition from total separation to deep involvement in world affairs and ambivalence over our sisters being involved in public issues. By the end of the decade, however, we had a clear affirmation from our congregational leaders and from one another that social activism is part of our call. We welcomed the pastoral letter *Justice in the World*, issued by the U.S. bishops in 1971. One statement reinforced our conviction that working for justice is not an optional pursuit but is integral to the gospel: "Action on behalf of justice and participation in the transformation of the world appear to us as a constitutive dimension of the preaching of the gospel, or, in other words, of the church's mission for the redemption of the human race and its liberation from every oppressive situation." We celebrated this liberating statement as a landmark.

Sisters participated in political caucuses and demonstrations, including vigils for slain civil rights workers and protests against the Vietnam War and the Gulf War. Some also protested Honeywell's production of cluster bombs. Sisters Char Madigan and Rita Foster were among the early organizers of nonviolent protests there. In the early 1990s when Honeywell moved its weapons making to Alliant Technical Systems in Hopkins, the protesters moved there, too. Several sisters took part in antiwar demonstrations protesting the U.S. bombing of Iraq, the sanctions on Iraq, and intervention in Yugoslavia.

Societal conditions and movements provided impetus for political action. Some sisters became active in the Civil Rights movement, which in the beginning was primarily concerned with voting rights of African Americans. The notion of civil rights soon expanded to include the right to be born, to be housed adequately, and to be employed. Civil rights further evolved to encompass Native Americans and other ethnic minorities, sexual minorities, and women.

The *Roe v. Wade* Supreme Court decision in 1973 legalizing abortion in every state brought our deep convictions about the sacredness of life to the forefront. As a community we support all efforts to reverence and enhance the life of each person from beginning to end. Some of us are active in the prolife movement. Others focus their energy on abolishing the death penalty. After Sister Helen Prejean, a Sister of St. Joseph from the Medaille congregation and a well-known author and advocate for abolishing the death penalty, spoke at a gathering of the Federation of Sisters of St. Joseph in St. Louis in 2000, the 1,550 sisters present released a public statement on their stand against capital punishment. Also in the summer of 2000 Sister Mary Mark Mahoney, retired for many years, and Sister Carol Neuburger testified at a court appeal in Oklahoma and tried, unsuccessfully, to commute the death sentence of a prisoner with whom Sister Mary Mark had been corresponding for three years. She continues her special ministry by corresponding with other prison "pen pals."

As we moved from convents and from institutions into neighborhoods, many of us became more involved in public issues. When some of us moved from the College of St. Catherine into neighborhood housing in 1968, the college's student publication, *The Catherine Wheel* (May 10, 1968, p. 8) described the experience as not a departure from traditional religious living but rather as an opportunity to open up new possibilities of religious life in the spirit of renewal.

Moving into different living situations brought us into new ministries and political involvement. In the mid-1970s, Sisters Jean Campbell and Jackie Slater moved into the Cedar-Riverside housing project in Minneapolis, a multiracial, multi-economic, integrated community. Sister Jackie's work there led her to run for the city council. She reported: "A few of the older and more traditional Catholics were upset about my candidacy for office. They were concerned that a nun would have a hard time in the nasty world of politics, or they were clinging to the notion that sisters should be either teachers or nurses. But there were also many who were very much in favor of it and they gave me their support and votes" (*Minneapolis Star Tribune*, December 24, 1977). Jackie won the election and became an influential as well as controversial council member. After her sudden death in 1984, the city of Minneapolis honored her by naming a renovated block of housing near downtown Minneapolis Slater Square.

Sister Jackie was not the first sister from the St. Paul Province to seek public office. Running on a prolife platform, Sister Elizabeth Regnier narrowly missed being elected to the North Dakota state legislature in 1972. Two years earlier in Jamestown, North Dakota, Sister Rose Alma Woychik lost the election to a ward precinct post by two votes.

While some sisters sought to influence public policy through elected office, Sister Mary Madonna Ashton received a state appointment from Minnesota Governor Rudy Perpich. During her tenure as Commissioner of Health from 1983 to 1991, Minnesota led the nation in addressing major health concerns by implementing tobacco control programs and HIV/AIDS prevention measures.

A number of us received our political initiation when Senator Eugene McCarthy from Minnesota sought the Democratic nomination for president in 1968. At the precinct caucus so many sisters showed up that we overwhelmed the proceedings. Some of us remember how upset the politician who chaired the meeting was when he saw all of us. Suspicious of the sisters' unaccustomed activism, he told us in no uncertain terms that he expected us to continue to come to the subsequent caucuses, and we did.

Some of us believed that protesting was part of our mission. In addition to her political involvement, Sister Rose Alma Woychik protested at missile bases in Jamestown, North Dakota, beginning in the mid-1960s. In a 1975 letter to Sister Frances Babb, she expressed the pivotal shift from suspicion of the world and withdrawal from it to wholehearted engagement with the world, which came to characterize the thinking of many sisters in the remaining decades of the twentieth century. She wrote: "I am not willing to admit that being interested in politics necessarily means that I am less interested in the love of God and my neighbor, or the spread of the gospel."

While some sisters protested against the Vietnam War and others demonstrated against legalized abortion, still others lobbied for fair housing, jobs, health care, education, and welfare legislation. Seeing government cuts in human services and increases in military spending, we insisted that enormous expenditures for weapons to protect the national security were creating havoc in our cities. As Sister Rita Steinhagen keeps saying, "One thing led to another." We did social analysis, asking who benefits and who suffers. We learned from our sisters in Peru that multinational success and security for developed countries meant tragic insecurity to the majority in developing countries.

When Sister Char Madigan began working in a downtown parish in the 1970s, she realized she was saying good night to people at 5:00 P.M. knowing they had no home to go to. Sisters Rita Steinhagen, Laura Geyer, and Char Madigan began offering shelter in their upper flat convent. That eventually led to the opening of St. Joseph's House, Ascension Place, and Incarnation House, all in Minneapolis, which were transitional housing shelters designed to empower women to live healthy, independent lives. In November 2000, Incarnation House began a new phase of service to women and children as it held an open house to celebrate its partnership with Wayside, a Minneapolis-based program designed to help women achieve their full potential and become productive members of the community.

Experience in these newly established shelters and runaway centers led Sister Marguerite Corcoran and three of the

Sister Marguerite Corcoran welcomes a friend to an open house at Incarnation House in 1994. Sister Marguerite founded a small card-making industry, Cottage Collective, where women living at Incarnation House learn the skills of designing and silk-screening cards for all occasions.

McDonald sisters, Rita, Brigid, and Jane, to question what was going on in the broader world community. A fourth McDonald sister, Kate, who along with others taught English to refugees and immigrants, had the same question. Her sister, Sister Brigid, while working at Incarnation House, connected us with Women Against Military Madness (WAMM) to pressure legislative bodies to direct government funds to welfare rights instead of to military spending. A growing interest in liberation theology, which focuses on the struggles of those who are poor and encourages religious people to champion nonviolent resistance, motivated many sisters to support WAMM's work.

Sisters have joined in solidarity with our Native American sisters and brothers seeking to preserve their cultural beliefs. At the invitation of Ojibwe elder woman Bea Swanson, Sister Jane McDonald helps staff an intergenerational and interracial prayer lodge at All Nations Church in Minneapolis. That experience led her to stand in solidarity with Native American struggles against land pollution—for example, the pollution of Prairie Island Indian land with the storing of nuclear waste. In the late 1990s Sisters Jane McDonald, Jan Dalsin, and Mary O'Brien and oth-

Sister Theresa O'Brien began her ministry among the Southeast Asian community in the mid-1980s. The Catholic Hmong community welcomed her into the Yang family and named her Poui Der Yang. She was blessed according to Hmong custom and received Hmong native dress. She is pictured here with Asian immigrants in St. Paul.

ers joined the Native American protest against a highway reroute that sacrificed sacred sites, including trees and spring-fed waters, for the sake of a highway expansion. Other sisters helped Native Americans adjust to urban life by providing basic necessities and connecting them with social service agencies.

For twenty years our sisters have worked with the Resource Center of the Americas and other Sanctuary movements, both for indigenous peoples in other lands and with refugees fleeing those lands. While serving as director of a sanctuary house in Waco, Texas, Sister Marie Richard King worked to provide temporary safe haven for undocumented persons from Mexico. Sisters have been arrested, and some imprisoned, for such "illegal" activities as supporting the César Chavez United Farm Workers grape boycott in 1968, standing with Salvadoran refugees who sought sanctuary in the Cathedral of St. Paul, and demonstrating against the manufacture of nuclear weapons. After more than twenty years of involvement in human rights issues, Sister Betty McKenzie connected sisters to the St. Paul Ecumenical Alliance of Churches (SPEAC), an ecumenical effort to work locally for housing, fair wages, and environmental issues.

The plight of persons who are homeless continues to be of deep concern to us. In one instance, both serendipity and providence played a part in the opening of an overnight shelter. Sister Dolore Rochon, an administrator at St. Joseph's Hospital in downtown St. Paul, was having coffee with Sister Rita Steinhagen one blizzardy December day in 1981. Sister Rita, then working at the nearby Dorothy Day Center, expressed concern that so many homeless people were sleeping in downtown doorways and in caves near the river. Sister Dolore, aware there was an empty floor in Mary Hall, the nurses' residence at the hospital, persuaded hospital and province leaders to convert this space into overnight housing for homeless persons. A week later, on New Year's Eve, with a wind chill of seventy degrees below zero, the doors of Mary Hall opened. Sisters volunteered to spend nights with the guests until Catholic Charities assumed responsibility for the residence.

Another dream became reality when Sister Rose Tillemans established Peace House, a space where people gather during the day for sharing and prayer. To her, Peace House is "one answer to the seldom looked-at question of what do the poor and disadvantaged do after they have some food, clothing, and shelter." She set up a storefront in 1985 on Franklin Avenue in Minneapolis, and since then people have come each day for coffee, food, and meditation. Together, they form community in a safe atmosphere built on acceptance, a sense of belonging, friendship, dignity, and mutuality of service.

Our commitment to supporting people who experience poverty, abuse, torture, mental illness, or discrimination remains strong. In Minneapolis, sisters are involved in INSTEP, a child care program that helps low-income parents pursue work and/or educational opportunities to become more self-sufficient. When the Derham Convent building in St. Paul became available in the 1990s, the province opened Sarah's

Sister Rose Tillemans (right) *joins a Peace House songfest directed by Sister Jane McDonald. Peace House provides a place for women and men who spend significant time on the streets to share companionship, conversation, food, and fun for a few hours each midday.*

Oasis, a temporary home for women, including refugees, some of whom come from the Center for the Victims of Torture in Minneapolis. At Sarah's women live in a safe environment that fosters relationships, reflection, and self-empowerment.

As a psychologist, Sister Karen Hilgers worked with many adult women who had survived abuse. She dreamed of a peaceful residence—not a hospital—where women in crisis could spend a few days with a supportive staff to regain their equilibrium. In collaboration with a small group of other psychologists Sister Karen developed this new approach to treatment. In 1996, Cornelia Place opened its doors in Minneapolis, providing the care and support the women needed. Although the model Sister Karen and her colleagues created proved to be a successful crisis management model, the residential portion of the program closed because of lack of funding. Cornelia Place now operates as a mental health clinic specializing in the treatment of women with posttraumatic stress disorder.

Through our experiences in pastoral and social ministries, we realized that unjust economic systems are significant factors leading to the oppression of people. This insight led Sister Mary Ellen Foster to complete a master's degree at the New School for Social Research in New York City, a school that critiques economic systems with an eye towards social transformation. Following her studies, Sister Mary Ellen began to teach classes in economics stressing the impact of economic systems on the world and urging her students to engage in activities that lead to systemic change.

Clearly, our concerns for social justice extend beyond the U.S. boundaries. Recognizing needs around the globe, sisters have responded in various ways. While Sister Florence Steichen served as registrar at Bethlehem University in the occupied West Bank, the Israeli military governor closed the university for three years because of the *Intifada*, the struggle of Palestinian young people to gain independence. Sister Florence played a major role in arranging for off-campus classes to help Palestinian students continue their education. She and other sisters who taught at Bethlehem University returned home with a commitment to further Palestinian rights by speaking, writing, contacting legislators, and seeking funds for Bethlehem University from our Partners in Justice fund. Continuing her advocacy for peace in the Middle East, Sister Florence works with Minnesota Middle East Peace Now and the Middle East Committee of Women Against Military Madness.

Representing our province at the United Nations Fourth World Conference on Women in Beijing in 1995, Sister Susan Oeffling learned firsthand about the status and plight of women throughout the world. While she was in Beijing, at the invitation of Minnesota Public Radio, Sister Susan called in regularly to report on the conference and answer listeners' questions. Upon returning home, she gave numerous talks on her Beijing experience to parish, school, corporate, and religious groups and published an article entitled "Keep on Keeping On" in *Sisters Today*. She joined the nonviolence working group of the Justice Commission, which then changed its name to Beyond Beijing: Women and Violence to focus on implementation of the Beijing platform.

As we struggled to "walk on the two feet of justice" in these last fifty years, we realized that we needed education and support in our efforts. As coordinator of the Social Justice Secretariat from 1979 to 1982, Sister Kathy Roehl kept us informed about justice issues and actions we could take to address the issues. We then established the Social Justice Task Force in 1982, which evolved into the Justice Commission in 1984. Sister Carol Neuburger, the first chair of the commission, brought energy and initiative to the work of justice. With her guidance, the province developed a process for sisters in the province to take a "corporate stand," that is, to make a public statement in the name of the Sisters of St. Joseph of the St. Paul Province. The process ensured that a corporate stand would represent the will of a majority of sisters, not a small group within the province. We took our first corporate stand in 1986 as a strong symbolic action for peace: "To declare as nuclear-free zones properties owned by the Sisters of St. Joseph in the St. Paul Province."

The province hired Joänne Tromiczak-Neid, a former Sister of St. Joseph, in 1992 as the full-time justice coordinator to help us address issues of social justice discussed at the congregational chapter and written in our Acts of Chapter. In addition to networking with local and national justice groups, Joänne was instrumental in starting Women Religious for

Justice, a collaborative effort of area religious communities. Among the founders of www.Sistersonline.org, a collaborative venture begun in 1996 with other communities of women religious in Minnesota, Joänne sees the website as facilitating outreach "to women and children who suffer from the multiple manifestations of injustice" (*Together*, November 1999, p. 13). As part of a global movement of women who care deeply about what is happening with the world, the earth, and its people, Sistersonline's 1999–2000 focus included debt relief and women in prison.

The role of women in the church is the concern of many of us. Sister Frances Babb, throughout her long life, was an ardent feminist. At the age of six in 1912, she handed out women's suffrage pamphlets with her mother. From the age of sixteen, she was certain that she had a vocation to the ordained priesthood, and throughout her life she was a persuasive spokeswoman for the ordination of women. In 1975 she spoke eloquently and painfully, with her commanding voice and strong Maine accent, of her desire to be a priest when she presented a petition to the official board for the Permanent Diaconate asking that the St. Paul and Minneapolis Archdiocese permit women to enter the Permanent Diaconate Training program. No action was taken on her petition.

Our first public efforts on behalf of gay, lesbian, bisexual, and transgendered (GLBT) persons were undertaken by Sister Sarah O'Neill, who dedicated much of her time and energy to seeking reconciliation and support between the Catholic Church and Catholic gays and lesbians. She worked tirelessly to assist with the founding of the Catholic Pastoral Committee on Sexual Minorities (CPCSM). In the years since Sister Sarah's death, some sisters have participated in demonstrations against repression of GLBT persons and sought to help families/friends both understand the church's position on GLBT persons and respect the individual's conscience. In June of 1999, twenty-two sisters and consociates marched in the Twin Cities Gay Pride Parade. They carried a large banner stating, "Sisters of St. Joseph of Carondelet, St. Paul, MN, Justice Commission, Standing for Human Rights and Justice." It was the first time we had walked in the parade so publicly.

As we look to the future, we recognize that the need to "walk on the two feet of justice" at times exceeds our ability to be involved personally and directly. In recent years we have found additional ways to support our quest for justice. After we sold St. John's Hospital in Fargo, North Dakota, we established the Giving Board in 1987, which allowed sisters to request grants for persons with immediate needs such as child care and living expenses. The sale of St. Mary's Hospital in Minneapolis presented us with a unique opportunity and challenged us to use the money generated to fulfill our mission. We developed a focus statement to guide our vision: "We, the community of the Sisters of St. Joseph [of the St. Paul Province], in keeping with our commitment to the gospel, choose, in dialogue with one another to use our spiritual, material, and personal resources in collaborative efforts to support those in need."

An Allocations Task Force recommended that the funding of ministries be spread across a range of categories representing a continuum of risk, from sponsored institutions and affiliated ministries to new, ongoing, or collaborative projects and individual radical responses to the gospel. As a result of the work of the task force, we established the Partners in Justice fund, which supports ministries that respond uniquely to unmet needs of the economically oppressed and to ministries that further our historical commitment to women and children.

Another vehicle for funding our ministries, the Partners in Ministry fund of our Ministries Foundation, "seeks to make a difference in the lives of those in need by generating and allocating funds to support present and future ministries of the Sisters of St. Joseph of Carondelet" (Ministries Foundation mission statement, 1995). Foundation board members, both sisters and laypeople, dedicate their time and efforts to ensuring that our mission and ministries continue into the future.

As we look back on the last fifty years we see how we have divided the city and sought to be attentive to the needs of our neighbors. Although, at times, tensions existed among us and we do not always agree on how to address the needs, we have grown in respect for one another as we realized that there are many ways to do the works of justice. Our Congregation of the Sisters of St. Joseph of Carondelet "encourages each sister [and consociate] to witness in areas of concern according to the dictates of an informed conscience and supports the rights of members to take a public stand on matters of justice" (Complementary Document 1984, p. 12). As needs continue to manifest themselves, we are confident that, like our foremothers, our sisters, consociates, and partners in ministry will divide the city and stand with the dear neighbor.

15

Moving Beyond Our Boundaries

T HE WORK OF OUR SISTERS in overseas missions has affected us both as individuals and as a province community.
Through the strength of their commitment, we can see
our lives in relationship to a larger world. Sisters send information home about their experiences, and when they return for
visits they talk in depth about the people they live among and
the impact of political, economic, and spiritual realities on daily
life. We are increasingly globally aware of the richness of
diverse cultures and hear how U.S. policies affect developing
countries. We also see, many times painfully, how the materialism and consumerism of our culture affects others. Above all,
we hear our sisters' pleas for world justice.

Our congregation began to reach out beyond our geographic boundaries in 1938, when the first sisters from the St.
Louis and Los Angeles Provinces went to Hawaii to teach. Some
years later the congregation sent sisters to Japan and Peru
and, more recently, to Chile. While initially we went to Japan
and Peru to teach young people or to nurse the sick, it was not
long before we found other challenges and saw our ministries
evolve to respond to new needs.

The first sisters from St. Paul went to "the islands" in
1946, eight years after the first sisters had begun the Hawaii
mission. Since then, thirty-seven sisters from the St. Paul
Province have taught in Hawaii, and they recall their early days

there as difficult. Some pastors were European and not accustomed to, or particularly accepting of, competent women as coworkers. Classes were very large—more than seventy pupils at times—and for many of them, English was not a first language. These students came from large plantation camps where the workers formed communities according to their ethnic culture: Filipino, Chinese, Japanese, Portuguese, Hawaiian, Samoan, Hispanic, Vietnamese, Korean, Cambodian, Laotian, Pacific Islander, or Caucasian. In addition to being in the classroom, sisters taught catechism at the U.S. military base, trained altar boys, and visited the imprisoned and the sick (including people with leprosy). Sister Agnes Iten, who returned to St. Paul in 2000 after twenty-three years in Hawaii, often acted as a tour guide for visitors to help explain the multicultural reality of Hawaii.

While teaching in Hawaii, Sister Miriam Shea visited pineapple fields where parents of her students worked to provide for their families.

In 1998, our sisters in Hawaii celebrated the sixtieth anniversary of the founding of the first mission of the Sisters of St. Joseph. At the time, Sister Kathleen Marie Shields, director of religious education for the Honolulu Diocese, wrote: "As we travel toward the third millennium, we experience a remarkable family resemblance to our pioneer sisters. Though our community life, ministries, and religious governance have changed dramatically over the sixty years, that spirit of gospel mobility and that tenacious love for our island people has deepened. We keep our eyes focused on the signs of the times, the emerging needs of our people, and the multicultural challenges surrounding us, just as we did six decades ago." Along with Sister Kathleen Marie, Sisters Marie Agnese Arsenault and Ann William Leach continue to minister in Hawaii.

Two sisters from the St. Paul Province, Sisters Sheila Sullivan and Barbara Mary Lamey, died in Hawaii and are buried there. Because of them we feel our presence among the people is permanent. In recent years, through our grants program, we have funded projects there such as the development of a cooperative, a mobile dental clinic, a food bank, and a counseling service.

Our mission in Japan began when Pope Pius XII asked religious communities in the United States to send missionaries to Japan or Africa. Sister Eucharista Galvin, then superior general, and her council decided that we would help by staffing a school for girls in Japan. The first four sisters, under the leadership of Sister Irmina Kelehan, a high school teacher and administrator in the St. Paul Province, arrived in Kyoto on August 15, 1956, and immediately began language study at the Naganuma Language School. After staying for two months with Sisters of St. Joseph of Wichita, Kansas, who had been in Japan for some years, the sisters moved into their Kyoto convent.

As future principal of the proposed school, Sister Irmina was responsible for determining the school's location. On the feast of St. Joseph in 1958, the ideal spot was found in nearby Tsu. One year later, St. Joseph Joshi Gakuen (St. Joseph's Girls School) opened there. The venture was a suitable one for the congregation, Sister Irmina said, because of the high regard for education in Japan. The school has an excellent academic reputation, and graduates from St. Joseph's enter the best universities in Japan—even the prestigious Tokyo University.

Sister Irmina Kelehan with several seniors at St. Joseph Joshi Gakuen.

Most of the students at the school are Buddhist but are enrolled by their parents because St. Joseph Joshi Gakuen offers moral and character development and a very strong program in English as a second language. From the beginning, teachers worked to instill Christian social principles in students. The religion course is an overview of Christianity with an emphasis on the life and meaning of Jesus. Students are expected to do volunteer work, and they regularly visit and help in nearby institutions for people who are blind, deaf, elderly, or mentally or physically disabled. The girls take part in an annual walkathon to raise money for people living in poverty in India and the Philippines.

Adapting to the Japanese culture, so strongly shaped by Buddhism and Shintoism, challenged the sisters from the very beginning. Small customs like using chopsticks, sitting on the floor, bowing, and trying not to be too blunt in expressing opinions were not problems. Even the food was not too difficult to adjust to, partly because of the ever-present rice. More difficult for the American sisters was the need to understand practices such as spending long hours in discussion on what seemed to them to be relatively minor matters. In Kyoto, the cultural capital of Japan, the sisters experienced many of the country's fine art forms: the tea ceremony, flower arranging, calligraphy, and the many customs and celebrations connected with the temples and shrines of the city.

Sister Marie Smith, who taught at St. Joseph Joshi Gakuen for thirty-five years, returned to Minnesota for two years to earn a master's degree in Japanese studies in the Department of Oriental Languages at the University of Minnesota. Back home in Minnesota today, she comments that Japanese and American sisters at times created almost a third culture through daily living together. Today, the native-born Japanese Sisters of St. Joseph of Carondelet in Japan outnumber those from the United States. Their work has expanded beyond the school in Tsu and now includes a variety of social ministries.

Just as our congregation responded to the call of Pope Pius XII to go to Japan, so did we respond to the call of Pope John XXIII, who invited religious communities to send missionaries to Latin America. Sister Eucharista Galvin, as superior general, visited Peru and deliberated possibilities with her council. They assigned nine sisters to educational work in Ica, Chimbote, and Arequipa who arrived in October 1962. In August of that year three sisters arrived as hospital personnel to serve in supervisory positions at Hospital Militar Central in Lima.

These sisters recognized the poverty and oppression of the majority of people. Concerned about the needs of the poor and the powerless, they left the hospital for ministries that allowed them to carry out our congregational option for the economically poor. Between 1972 and 1974 two sisters moved to a Chimbote pueblo *joven* (new town) where very poor people lived. In the mountain areas of Moho and Ocobamba they established two new houses and in Ica, Arequipa, Lima, and Chimbote began ministries in poor neighborhoods.

The chaos of terrorism that began in 1980 affected our sisters greatly. The Ocobamba ministry had to be closed in

1983, and Moho was closed for a year. Death threats for some sisters caused them to move and even to leave the country. The terrorism is now reduced, although the Peruvian elections in 2000, and the public scandals that followed them, once again intensified political uncertainty in Peru.

Currently, three sisters from St. Paul minister in Peru. Sister Patricia McHale offers spiritual direction and retreats to people in Lima, and Sister Kathleen Judge is a parish leader among the Aymara people in Puno. Sister Lilly Long, who began her ministry there in 1999, works as a clinic nurse and parish worker in Arequipa. Sister Patricia, who has been in Peru since 1962, says that our per-sonal and communal con-cern for the poor "orients our choice of ministries and our lifestyle as we try to exemplify love, the only sign which Jesus gave us."

Sister Patricia McHale visits with a Peruvian mother and her two children.

Today the number of native Peruvian Sisters of St. Joseph of Carondelet is equal to the number of North American sisters serving in the country. Their ministries include running communal kitchens, offering medical services in clinics, providing a center for working children, helping at a city orphan-age, and serving as pastors in parishes. They also prepare litur-gies and teach religious education in public schools. Their major goal is to help small Christian communities to grow.

In 1986, the sesquicentennial anniversary year of the 1836 establishment of the Sisters of St. Joseph in the United

States, our congregation responded to a request of Bishop Don Carlos of Talca, Chile. The membership of the entire congregation discerned the feasibility of establishing a mission in Chile. Like much of Latin America, Chile was suffering from military oppression and social disintegration. There was no question among us about the need for a religious community to minister with the poor in Talca. Furthermore, because of the threatening situation in Peru with the *Sendero Luminoso* terrorists, it seemed prudent to have another location in Latin America if the sisters in Peru should be forced to seek refuge. Don Carlos's only advice to us was, "Live among my people. Get to know them. When they trust you, they will ask you to share in their lives and ministry."

Sister Rose Mary Haley, who had earlier ministered in Peru, was among the first four sisters from the congregation who opened the Chilean mission in December 1987. Their house was located in the parish of San Sebastian in the Carlos Trupp sector of Talca, a developing and impoverished housing area for some 5,000 newly arrived families. The pastor of the parish had earlier written to our sisters: "I would ask you to become poor people in the midst of the poor. You must not fall into the temptation of the 'pastoral of the dollar.' Observe how the people act. They share the little they have (a spoonful of oil, a little sugar). You must do the same. If not, from the first day you will have a line of clients, but you will never have brothers and sisters."

Little by little, the sisters began to "divide the city" and take responsibility for particular situations. They set up a small dispensary, taught reading to adults, did catechetical work with mentally and physically disabled youngsters, and joined the women in the *comedor*, a common kitchen–dining room where food is prepared and served. They gave help to people with the disease of alcoholism, the number-one health concern in the country. At Casa Belen (House of Bethlehem), they provide a caring home and social services for young girls who are developmentally disabled. In San Sebastian parish sisters helped establish a well-equipped library and cultural center for the people.

One year after the mission in Talca was opened, our sisters, including Sister Mary Joseph Wilson from the St. Paul Province, established a seond house in Curepto, an old sixteenth-century European settlement. Curepto is the center of municipal, economic, and religious life for some 3,000 people living in town and about 8,000 people living in the surrounding rural area. For the majority, who are very poor, there are only limited and part-time opportunities for work.

Sisters not wearing habits or having a mother superior were a new experience for the townspeople. The fact that the *Hermanas* (sisters) were not going to reopen the parish school or staff the municipal hospital left the people free, as one

Sister Mary Joseph Wilson (second from right) *works with other women to prepare food for a neighborhood celebration in Talca, Chile.*

woman said, "to come to the sisters for anything." And people came—even a thief, who made off with all of the houseplants in the convent.

In recent years, more sisters have left than have come to the mission in Chile. But the work continues, and as the Chileans always add, *si Dios quiere* (if God wishes it), the mission will endure.

Through our sisters who have served in Hawaii, Japan, Peru, and Chile we have received the blessing of coming to know sisters from other provinces. We can talk with each other about the mission of our congregation as being rooted in the love of God and neighbor.

Other sisters from the St. Paul Province have gone beyond our borders for ministries not directly sponsored by the congregation. Five have served as Peace Corps volunteers. When Sister Isabella Ferrell studied in Africa as a Fulbright scholar, she was so affected by the poverty of the country's educational system that she returned to Africa to teach at the National Education School in Libreville, Gabon. Sister Maria Wilson spent three years in Costa Rica, where she lived with families and taught arts and crafts to local women to help them sustain themselves.

Three sisters from the congregation of the Sisters of St. Joseph of Nazareth-on-the-Lake served in the Peace Corps before their congregation merged with the St. Paul Province in 1986. Sister Laura King's childhood dream of visiting the Far East came true when she went to Malaysia, where for four years she taught math and language to junior high school students. Although she had hoped to go to South America or the Philippines, Sister Geraldine Biron was assigned to Ethiopia. She asked herself, "Why not?" and went to work at the Harar Institute near Addis Ababa. She helped train future teachers and, at the same time, studied the native language. Sister John

Berchmans Mullay later joined Sister Geraldine in Ethiopia as a Peace Corps volunteer; earlier she had served in the Philippines. In both countries, she taught young people.

Sisters who have worked around the world emphasize the need for a conscious choice to live simply when involved in another culture. Each of us is enriched vicariously by the people among whom our sisters live and the customs and history in which they are immersed. Further, their experiences change us and encourage us to reach out to people from diverse world cultures living in our own backyards.

Our congregational chapter of 1997 challenges us to recognize the incarnation of Jesus Christ as the most powerful model of inculturation (Philippians 2:6–7) and to commit ourselves more deeply to understanding and experiencing multicultural realities. We are to try to be open and welcoming to people of all races and cultures, always aware of our need for continual conversion. Like our first sisters in Le Puy, we face our future with trust in the God who has called us to keep our eyes open on the whole world.

"Continual Joy of Spirit"

Contributors

In addition to the names listed here, many other Sisters of St. Joseph, consociates, and former members were a part of this project through interviews and informal recollections.

Mary Madonna Ashton, Aline Baumgartner, Margaret Belanger, Clare Blanchette, Vera Chester, Elaine Conrad, Nancy Cosgriff (former member), Roland Davey, Mary Margaret Deeney, Katherine Egan, Joanne Emmer, Agnes Foley, Kathleen Foley, Mary Ellen Foster, Roseann Giguere, Betty Ann Gits, Agatha Grossman, Marie Grossman, Susan Hames, Mary Ann Hanley, Mary Hasbrouck, Mary Heinen, Karen Hilgers, Ansgar Holmberg, Sharon Howell, Alberta Huber, Carmen Shaughnessy Johnson (consociate), Joan Kain, Judith Kavanaugh, Karen Kennelly, Mary Kessler, Mary E. Kraft, Lucy Knoll, Margaret Kvasnicka, Mary Lamski, Mary Lang, Shirley Lieberman (consociate), Eleanor Lincoln, Catherine Litecky, Char Madigan, Shawn Madigan, Katherine McLaughlin, Catherine McNamee, Mary Kaye Medinger (consociate), Joan Mitchell, Patrice Neuberger, Bernadette Newton, Andre Nilles, Kristen Furth Neufeld (former member), Susan Oeffling, Marie de Paul Rochester, Genevieve Schillo, Angela Schreiber, Marie Herbert Seiter, Marie T. Smith, Florence Steichen, Linda Taylor, Virginia Webb, Mary Joseph Wilson, Jean Wincek, John Christine Wolkerstorfer

The following people reviewed an early draft of the book and made helpful comments and suggestions: Sisters St. Luke Copeland, Constance Marie DeFoe, Katherine Egan, Chris Ludwig, Susan Oeffling, Dolore Rochon, and Ann Walton; consociate Deborah Chernik; and friends of the province Jane Keefe Clifford, Reverend John Gilbert, Mary Jo Richardson, and Ann Thompson.

Bibliography

The major sources for this book are to be found in the St. Paul Province Archives. Contributors have also relied on interviews and their own lived experience.

Coburn, Carol and Martha Smith. *Spirited Lives: How Nuns Shaped Catholic Culture and American Life, 1836–1920.* Chapel Hill: The University of North Carolina Press, 1999.

Flannery, Austin, ed. *Vatican Council II: The Conciliar and Post Conciliar Documents.* Northport, NY: Costello Publishing, 1988.

Hurley, Helen Angela. *On Good Ground: The Story of the Sisters of St. Joseph in St. Paul.* Minneapolis: University of Minnesota Press, 1951.

Murphy, Ellen. *Body of Time.* [St. Paul:] North Central Publishing, [1971].

Nepper, Marius. *Origins: The Sisters of St. Joseph.* 1969 translation, 3d printing. Wichita, KS: Acme Lithographers, 1981.

Oeffling, Susan. "Keep on Keeping On." *Sisters Today*, March 1996, pp. 94–99.

Raiche, Annabelle. *A Home Becomes a College: St. Paul Diocesan Teachers College, 30 Years in the James J. Hill Mansion.* St. Paul: Good Ground Press, 2000.

Raiche, Annabelle and Ann Marie Biermaier. *They Came to Teach*. St. Cloud, MN: North Star Press, 1994.

Roach, John R. "For Real Leadership, Women's Voices Shouldn't Be Ignored," *The Catholic Spirit*, August 31, 2000, p. 11.

Ryan, Rosalie and John Christine Wolkerstorfer. *More Than a Dream: Eighty-five Years at the College of St. Catherine*. St. Paul: The College of St. Catherine, 1992.

Sampson, Ann Thomasine. *The History of St. Agatha's Conservatory of Music and Art*. St. Paul: St. Joseph Provincial House, 1984.

Sanger, Gregory. *All God's Children Have Brains*. Bryn Mawr, PA: Dorrance and Company, 1987.

Schwalen, Ursula. *Called . . . and Re-Called to Serve: The Story of the Sisters of St. Joseph of Nazareth-on-the-Lake, Superior, Wisconsin*. [Privately printed.]

Schwalen, Ursula. "Looking Back That Others Might Look Forward," *Review for Religious*, July/August 1990, pp. 553–66.

Smith, Maris Stella [Alice Gustava]. *Frost for St. Brigid*. New York: Sheed and Ward, 1949.

Smith, Maris Stella [Alice Gustava]. *Here Only a Dove*. Patterson, NJ: St. Anthony Guild Press, 1939.

Smith, Alice Gustava. *Collected Poems*. St. Paul: College of St. Catherine Alumnae Association, 1992.

Stoughton, Mary Judith. *Proud Donkey of Schaerbeek, Ade Bethune, Catholic Worker Artist*. St. Cloud, MN: North Star Press, 1988.

Sweeney, Helen Dolores. *Older Than Trees*. [n.p.], 1984.

Wolkerstorfer, John Christine. *"You Shall Be My People": A History of the Archdiocese of St. Paul and Minneapolis*. Strasbourg—France: Editions du Signe, 1999.

Other studies by/about Sisters of St. Joseph of Carondelet presenting the history of the St. Paul Province (all in St. Paul Province Archives):

Cantwell, Laurent. *A Design for Living: A History of the Sisters of St. Joseph in the Northwest*. St. Paul: North Central Publishing Company, 1973.

Communications Department. *History of St. Joseph's Hospital, St. Paul, Minnesota 1853–1978*. St. Paul: St. Joseph's Hospital, 1979.

Dougherty, Dolorita Marie, ed. *Sisters of St. Joseph of Carondelet*. St. Louis and London: B. Herder Book Company, 1966.

Graham, Clara. *Works to the King: Reminiscences of Mother Seraphine Ireland*. St. Paul: North Central Publishing Company, 1950.

Martens, Elizabeth Marie. *Academy for a Century: A History of Saint Joseph's Academy Located in Saint Paul, Minnesota*. St. Paul: North Central Publishing Company, 1951.

O'Brien, Antonine. *Heritage: A Centennial Commemoration: The Sisters of Saint Joseph of Carondelet 1836–1936*. St. Paul: College of St. Catherine, [1937].

Sampson, Ann Thomasine. *Care with Prayer: The History of St. Mary's Hospital and Rehabilitation Center, Minneapolis, Minnesota, 1887–1987*. Minneapolis: St. Mary's Hospital and Rehabilitation Center, 1987.

Sampson, Ann Thomasine. *Seeds on Good Ground: Biographies of 16 Pioneer Sisters of St. Joseph of Carondelet.* St. Paul: Sisters of St. Joseph of Carondelet, St. Paul Province, 2000.

Savage, Mary Lucinda, compiler. *The Century's Harvest.* Gathered by the Sisters of St. Joseph of Carondelet in the United States, 1836–1936. [St. Louis: n.p., 1936.]